Caught in the Path

Carolyn Blenn Barwer

Caught in the Path

The Fury of a Tornado
The Rebirth of a Community

By
Carolyn Glenn Brewer

PRAIRIE FUGUE BOOKS
LEATHERS PUBLISHING

KANSAS CITY, MISSOURI

Published by Leathers Publishing
4500 College Boulevard, Overland Park, Kansas 66211

Prairie Fugue Books
1283 W. 71st Terrace, Kansas City, Missouri 64114

Printed in the United States of America

For additional copies, write to:
Prairie Fugue Books
1283 W. 71st Terrace, Kansas City, Missouri
or call
(816) 444-3558

ISBN 0-9655774-0-6
LCCN 96-092889

"Between the earth and man arose the leaf.

Between the heaven and man came the cloud."

— *John Ruskin*

TABLE OF CONTENTS

FATALITY LIST

Within the first forty-eight hours, thirty-nine people were reported dead. Over the years, five more died from their tornado related injuries.

Isham Davis   Spring Hill, Kansas
Barbara Davis   Spring Hill, Kansas
Pamela Davis   Spring Hill, Kansas
Tamera Davis   Spring Hill, Kansas
Mrs. J.A. Marsh   Ottawa, Kansas
J.A. Marsh   Ottawa, Kansas
Lowell Atkinson   Martin City
Margaret Erlene Smith   Martin City
Joseph Vinchier   Grandview
Randall McGill   Grandview
Edward S. Henton   Grandview
Bessie Knorpp Smith near Richards-Gebaur Air Force Base
Gladys Erwin   Hickman Mills
Linda Sue Stewart   Hickman Mills
Gladys Taylor   Hickman Mills
Caroline Kay Taylor   Hickman Mills
Cornelia Davis   Hickman Mills
Katherine Sue Davis   Hickman Mills
Marjorie Wackernagle   Hickman Mills
Oral Glenn Hower   Hickman Mills
John Hower   Hickman Mills
Lena Rucker   Hickman Mills
Gerald Rucker   Hickman Mills
Dorothy Lavonne Leopold   Hickman Mills
Harold Keith Leopold   Hickman Mills
Charles Johnston   Ruskin Heights
Catherine Armon   Ruskin Heights
Alta Guyll   Ruskin High School
George Kildow   Ruskin High School
Robert W. Yost, Jr.   Ruskin Heights
Diane Boyd   Ruskin Heights
Hester Timm   Ruskin Heights
Denise Woodling   Ruskin Heights
Maxine Nehring   Ruskin Heights
Jeanette Nelson Dorris   Ruskin Heights
Arthur Frechette   northeast of Ruskin Heights
Charles Thompson   south of Ruskin Heights
Maybelle Gabbert   Raytown Road
Henry Gabbert   Raytown Road

This book is dedicated to their families.

AERIAL PHOTOGRAPH

The Path

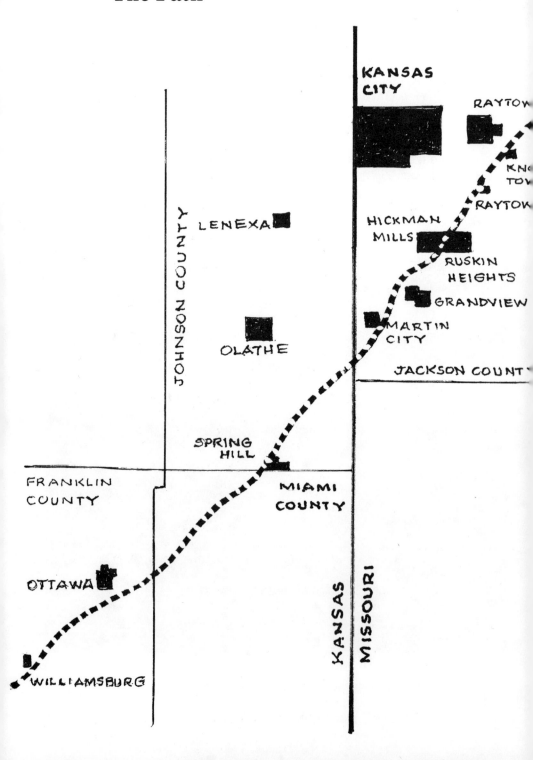

PHOTOGRAPHS

Front cover photo: May 20, 1957 tornado, Spring Hill, Kansas, taken by Rev. Robert Alexander, by permission of Marilyn Palmer, *courtesy of Tim Janicke*

Back cover photo: Russ Millin's house, *Russ Millin's private collection*

Aerial view, looking northeast of Hickman Mills and Ruskin Heights, *Bill Martin's private collection*

Model "D" Ruskin house, *author's private collection*

Our lot, summer of 1954, *author's private collection*

Hickman Mills, *Bill Martin's private collection*

Hembree house, *Anna Lee Hembree's private collection*

Hickman Mills looking east, *Bill Martin's private collection*

Kotsifakis basement, *Bill Martin's private collection*

Hickman Mills Bank, *Bill Martin's private collection*

Mennonites, *Bill Martin's private collection*

Ruskin Center, *Bill Martin's private collection*

Front hall closet in Ruskin home, *Bill Martin's private collection*

Ruskin Center A&P, *Bill Martin's private collection*

Austin Shute's house, *Austin Shute's private collection*

Kitchen sink, *Bill Martin's private collection*

Sea of debris, *Austin Shute's private collection*

Our house, *author's private collection*

McNamara's car, *author's private collection*

My dad's car, *author's private collection*

Ruskin Center, *E.J. and Jean Frounfelter's private collection*

Jean Frounfelter and her piano, *E.J. and Jean Frounfelter's private collection*

Ruskin Junior High, *E.J. and Jean Frounfelter's private collection*

Ruskin High School Gymnasium, *E.J. and Jean Frounfelter's private collection*

Frounfelter's house, *E.J. and Jean Frounfelter's private collection*

Jean McCoy in her kitchen, *Bob and Jean McCoy's private collection*

Debris pit, *E.J. and Jean Frounfelter's private collection*

Burke Elementary School, *E.J. and Jean Frounfelter's private collection*

"I'm all shook up," *Bob and Jean McCoy's private collection*

Unclaimed cars, *Floyd Zullig's private collection*

Resident Disaster Card, *author's private collection*

Memorial dedication, *Bill Martin's private collection*

ACKNOWLEDGMENTS

When I began research for this book my plan was to interview the friends and former neighbors of my parents. I meant to write the story of how a neighborhood survives disaster. But as my list of interviews grew longer, and more and more names came my way, I saw that the path of this storm cut deeply into the collective memory of the entire region. The stories were far too rich to limit them to a single neighborhood. There was, however, no way to contact everyone who was touched by the tornado. For every story told here there are dozens untold.

This book would have remained an idea if not for the generosity of those who shared their stories with me. My heartfelt thanks go to all who opened their homes to me. As they candidly told family stories, we laughed, drank coffee,cried together, and stripped back layers of memory to the raw core of that night. I admire their courage as much as I appreciate their hospitality.

Whenever possible, individual entries are verbatim from taped or telephone interviews. Without changing the content or spirit of the conversation, I have sometimes edited for clarity.

Many others helped me blow the dust off research materials: Jean Hendershot at the Mid-Continent Library; Ruskin Heights Homes Association officers Julia Witty Caudle and Rick Hammer; Donna Swischer at the Linda Hall Library who never stopped with what the computer told her was available; the librarians at the Kansas City Public Library Missouri Valley Room; Anne Chiarelli Jones at the Johnson County Museum; all the librarians at the Jackson County Historical Society; Fred Ostby, John Halmsted, and Hugh Crowther of the National Severe Storm Forecast Center; Kitty Serling at Menorah Hospital Library; Dee Stenger and Major Brian Merritt of the Salvation Army; Sandy Feeler and Betty Dawson of the American Red Cross; Dave Boutros at the Western Historical Manuscript Collection at UMKC; Wendy Ramirez at the Ruskin Heights Presbyterian Church; Sandra Killion Duffelmeyer at the Ruskin Heights Baptist Church; the staff of the Truman Library; Wayside Waifs; Judy Hart at the Ozanam Home; Jeff Staake at the Missouri Department of Health; Sidney Bates and Fern Welch at the Kansas City Health Department; Linda Peters at St. Joseph Hospital; Dan Davidson at Menorah Hospital; Chuck Haddick at the Marr Sound Archives of UMKC; Lou Davis, for his help remembering the early days of Ruskin Heights; Steve Binns and Bernadette Hoyt, for proof-reading; and Frank Medina Sr. and Tom Leathers and his staff for all their generous advice.

I was very fortunate to have access to private photographs. Bill Martin's photographic documentation of his journey that first twenty-four hours became a story in itself. Others who provided me with photographs were E.J. and Jean Frounfelter, Bob and Jean McCoy, Anna Lee Hembree, Austin Shute, Peggy McNamara , Floyd Zullig, and Russ Millin. I'd also like to thank Marilyn Palmer for allowing me to use her father's photograph of the tornado and to Tim Janicke for providing that photo. The home movies of Gordon and Shirley Gross and Art and Ernestine Peterson brought the scenes to life and evoked my own memories.

My special thanks go to Jim and Aggie Turnbaugh for opening the archives of the *Jackson County Advocate* to me. Those great old volumes of actual newspapers held a wealth of information about the area while evoking the feel of 1957.

I was fortunate to hear tapes of Walt Bodine's radio show, *Diary of a Disaster,* produced within a week of the tornado. Because the edge of fear and horror remained in the voices of those he interviewed, they presented me with an invaluable contribution.

My thanks and gratitude to all the friends who encouraged me, even though I bombarded them with tornado stories. Their fresh eyes and ears helped me keep my perspective. Of those, I'd especially like to thank Mike Metheny, whose careful editing was much appreciated.

Most of all, I thank my family for never complaining about my self-imposed schedules and for supporting me in all ways. Lastly, with love, I thank my husband Tim, for his creative intuition.

PART I

PATH'S BEGINNING

I

In 1957 a tornado destroyed my home. Like a sinister alien it dropped out of a troubled May sky and twisted its way into our lives forever. I was seven years old and didn't know what a tornado was. I had heard the word at school only the week before, but it was an abstract word, with no frame of reference surrounding it. Then on that muggy night in May we survived our thirty seconds of terror. Afterwards my parents sat my five-year-old brother and me down on the kitchen table. My dad went across the street to help rescue a woman while my mother looked for shoes in the rubble that had only a few minutes before been our household possessions. Now I heard that awesome word echoing from adult to adult. I looked at my brother and wailed, "This is a tornado?" We both burst into tears.

Tornado had many definitions after May 20, 1957: horror, pain, death, plus an incomprehensible tangle of personal business and the frustrating annoyance of reorganizing one's life. But it also came to mean faith, courage and a deep sense of community resurrected out of the rubble, connecting all who shared that anxious night.

Those of us who found ourselves in the tornado's path have told our stories over and over again. At block parties and school reunions the subject inevitably comes up. Every spring we stare out office windows at churning skies and remind our coworkers that it can happen here. We tell the stories to our children, so that the tornado's path burrows deeper into our family histories. As with any catastrophic event, legends intertwine with truth, making a fabric of communal experience.

Anyone who lived in the Kansas City metropolitan area then has a memory of that night. Even those not directly affected have a story ready when I mention my tornado research. One long-time friend told me his Kansas City, Kansas Boy Scout troop visited stricken Ruskin Heights that summer as a field trip. Another friend said she would never forget the tornado date. Her sister was born that day, and her mother, who was a nurse, wanted to get out of her hospital bed to help the incoming tornado victims. I've heard stories of high school students in Independence giving up their lunch money so they could contribute to the Ruskin High School building fund, and of station-wagon owners enlisted as ambulance drivers.

I've often found myself drawn to the John Steuart Curry painting, Tornado. A whitish green funnel approaches a midwestern farm house, and I wonder what the children in the painting were doing earlier that day. What favorite toy did they leave behind as they scurried into the storm cellar? I understand the confusion on the little girl's face and the clenched white face of the mother. What was left of their life when it was all over?

What I know now is that it is never completely over. My neighborhood was rebuilt within six months, and after a time most of the neighbors moved away, taking their memories with them. Over the years most of the pain faded, leaving a residue of thankfulness. But the total experience of tornado is still with us. The smell of ozone during a summer storm, the shreds of insulation found between pages of a childhood book remind us that the tornado left a bit of itself with us, making it ours.

Few knew, on that sultry afternoon in May, that the story had already begun. People all over the city did what they always did on Monday afternoon. There was no reason to think this day was any different. It was unusually windy and the air did feel heavy and close, but after the thunderstorms of the past week, that was not surprising. It was nice not to have rain; children played outside at recess, lunches were eaten outside, laundry hung on clotheslines. It was a typical late spring day in the Midwest. Most didn't give a thought at all to the weather.

Joe Audsley and his colleagues at the National Severe Storm Forecast Center were the exceptions as they watched a storm system develop hundreds of miles west of the Kansas City metro area. It had already been a busy spring for the NSSFC. Located in Kansas City since 1954, the NSSFC tracked 300 tornadoes during the first four months of 1957 alone. The month of May produced another 324, the highest recorded number to date in a single month. This particular Monday afternoon proved to be a hectic one for weathermen. The first tornado of the day was sighted in eastern Colorado around eleven AM. As the afternoon wore on, the NSSFC followed storms in Oklahoma, Nebraska and Kansas, constantly updating and revising tornado information.

All along tree-lined streets of the quiet residential community of Hickman Mills, children played after-school games of hopscotch and jump rope, organized pick-up games of baseball and rode bikes. South of the Kansas City limits, Hickman Mills was founded as a trading post along the Santa Fe Trail and was proud of its hundred-year history. Descendants of the original families were still in the area and most could tell stories of a young Harry Truman helping with pig inoculations and working on threshing crews. But on this afternoon residents were working in their yards and enjoying their families.

Just east of Hickman Mills, in a new subdivision called Ruskin Heights, Treva Woodling got her house ready for a wedding shower she was giving her sister the next evening. After a downtown shopping trip with her mother-in-law, her four-year-old daughter, Diane, asked if she could spend the night at her grandmother's. The women decided another night would be more convenient.

In a small Missouri community, just a few miles southwest of the Hickman Mills area, there was plenty of excitement, but not about the weather. The kindergarten class of Martin City School planned to graduate that night. Half the town knew someone in that class.

In Ruskin Heights, high school principal Blaine Steck also had graduation on his mind. Commencement was scheduled for Tuesday, May 21, in the high school's new gym. Although everything was ready, he planned to return to the school that evening to go over last-minute details with the school board president and meet with the school nurse.

Dr. Alexander Shifrin relaxed at home with his family after a busy Monday at Menorah Hospital in Kansas City, where he was an internist. He had to return to the hospital for evening rounds, but he didn't expect that to take long.

A block and a half down the street from the high school, I was home from school recuperating from my annual bout of tonsillitis. Although we could count on my susceptibility to strep, my parents were reluctant to have my tonsils removed. They were still afraid of polio. My brother and I had been vaccinated but the vaccine was still too new to be sure of the long range protection. Large groups of children, including pediatric wards, were avoided.

By late afternoon, my mother felt I was well enough to go to my piano lesson. We drove the fifteen miles to my aunt's house for the lesson, then back home, stopping at the Ruskin Center A&P on the way. I remember getting a sucker in the checkout line, but not feeling well enough to want it. I just wanted to go back to bed. I was sound asleep by seven o'clock.

By dinner time, those who listened to the radio or had the television on knew the Kansas City area was in danger of "tornadic activity." Some were more interested in the A's starting line up against the Tigers that night than any weather information. Others hurried with dinner so they could watch *I Love Lucy*. As dusk quietly spread its serenity from the east, the communities of Martin City, Hickman Mills, and Ruskin Heights settled into the comfort of families and relaxation.

Time seemed to pause, marking this suspension as the last moment between peace and tragedy. Lives would never be the same. Even as my parents kissed me good night, all of nature's fury heaved itself into that western ground. The tornado was headed our way.

Storms frequently left their mark on this otherwise peaceful corner of southwestern Jackson County. The early settlers watched ominous clouds drape themselves across the horizon every spring, and by the time E.A. Hickman built his mill along the Santa Fe Trail area farmers already knew that high winds and hail were as common as the blooming of red buds and dogwoods. Many a squall line sliced through a lazy summer afternoon. Eyes turned to the southwest on those days sometimes saw funnel clouds playing a sinister game of hide and seek. Occasionally one would dip to the ground to destroy a barn or frighten the livestock.

Long known as part of Tornado Alley, this region is the country's most prolific incubator for such storms. As warm, muggy, unstable air is pulled inland from the Gulf of Mexico and collides with cold air cresting over the Rockies, severe storms are often formed. If high jet-stream winds are added, a counterclockwise spinning of air is set in motion horizontally, then vertically, as the storm builds. Warm ground temperatures of the afternoon and evening add to the mix as this surface layer air rises. Like a monstrous alchemist brew, these thunderstorms boil up thousands of feet. This kind of storm is capable of producing as much energy as a hydrogen bomb. Some spawn tornadoes.

Twice before, on May 30, 1879 and May 23, 1946, tornadoes touched down in southern Jackson County. Referred to as the "cyclone" in old county records, the 1879 tornado first struck near Raymore, Missouri and moved northeast through Lee's Summit, Blue Springs, and Buckner, sounding "like the roar of artillery" and destroying farm houses and out buildings with the "grasp of a giant." Six people were killed. The tornado plowed through the farmland "like a steamboat through water," caused tremendous crop damage, uprooted trees that looked as if they had been burned, and dropped thick mud everywhere. There were reports of a fireball leading the tornado's way.

The 1946 storm passed to the west of Hickman Mills, but battered Martin City. Debris from a Martin City fruit market, a silo, chicken houses and various parts of houses and barns all swirled in a furious mass toward the northeast. A giant elm tree from the Methodist churchyard in the center of town lay uprooted on the church steps like a macabre offering.

This tornado's worst damage centered in a community called Holmes Park, between U.S. Highway 71 and Hillcrest Road, along Bannister Road. Although the twister's path was narrow, a husband and wife were killed when their home smashed into another building. At nearby Benjamin Stables a barn turned on its foundation. The twenty-six horses inside turned right along with it and landed uninjured.

These tornadoes, like the one in May 1957, were part of a large system of tornadoes that broke out in Kansas and Missouri. The 1879 path extended eighty-six miles; the 1946, approximately ten miles. Because of the sparsely populated area they covered, few lives were lost, and the communities suffered a minimal amount of disruption. The next time the story would be different.

In early 1952 the Whitely estate, a large tract of land just east of Hickman Mills, became available for development. Hickman Mills residents understood that new land owners planned to build cozy Cape Cod houses on half acre lots. But before those owners drew out the plans the land was again sold, this time to the Praver brothers of New York.

The mood of the country was one of expansion. Everyone was tired of pinching pennies and worrying about depression or war. In the fifties, bigger was better. Skirts were worn longer and fuller. Cars were long and sleek with lots of chrome and fins. In business, franchising gained popularity and advertisers, especially on television, told us every day what we needed to make our American Dream complete. There were more things to buy and America was in a buying mood after two decades of struggle.

As the country converted from wartime rationing to a consumer economy some procedures learned from necessity benefited the general public. Inventions such as radar were easily adapted to civilian use by the Weather Bureau. Medical methods perfected in South Pacific jungles or field hospitals in Europe saved lives here as well.

Nowhere were new techniques more successfully applied than in the housing industry. As more young families moved away from urban areas there was a demand for affordable housing in the new suburbs. Many of these families were those of servicemen waiting to take advantage of a new G.I. home loan. Levittown, the prototype for this kind of bedroom community, was the brainchild of William Levitt, who in 1946 bought acres of potato farms on Long Island for development. Levitt's assembly-line type of production allowed workmen to go from house to house doing just one task. By 1955, seventy-five percent of all housing starts were in communities like this.

This was what the Pravers planned to build. They saw G.I.s who had outgrown their first apartments and wanted to raise their baby-boom families away from the city. They saw a planned community with room allowed for shopping areas, parks, schools and churches. The nearby Richards-Gebaur Air Force Base and the Bendix defense plant provided a potential ready-made population. Once people saw what could be built in those wheat fields, it would become their dream too.

The first object was to keep cost down. Using Levittown techniques, whole blocks were constructed at once. There was no room for customizing. The Pravers felt that by offering four styles—two-bedroom, three-bedroom, three-bedroom with basement, three bedroom with crawl space— there was something for everyone. All homes came with a patio, a garage and a den that could be used as an extra bedroom. A stove, refrigerator and washing machine were thrown into the deal as added incentive. Four model homes were set up on Blue Ridge Boulevard just south of the high school, and block by block the community of Ruskin Heights took form.

People loved these houses, the first of their kind in the Kansas City area. They were efficiently laid out: kitchen and dining area in the front, living room and den in the back and a long hallway leading to the bedrooms. Basement models were usually at either end of the block and sometimes one or two others in between. There was plenty of room in the backyard for a swing set, sand box and room for landscaping as well. Sycamore Park, within easy walking distance, gave the kids a larger play area and mothers a central place to visit. Houses were sold before they were built. Young couples with one or two children, maybe another on the way, couldn't wait to move in.

All this concerned some older Hickman Mills residents on the other side of Blue Ridge. Where would all these children go to school? Since 1901, when the school district became the first to consolidate in the state of Missouri, the same four grade schools had served the community. The Jackson County superintendent of schools at the time, William H. Johnson, had petitioned tirelessly to consolidate his home district and was given the honor of naming the high school that united the grade schools. Ruskin, named after English essayist and educator John Ruskin, opened its doors to twenty-five students in the fall of 1902. By the 1930s, the small school was overcrowded so a large two-story brick building was built a mile south. This new Ruskin High School, closer to Hickman Mills, sat proudly on a summit along the east side of Blue Ridge and the Kansas City Southern railroad line. A landmark among treeless fields, it became a hub of activity, pulling students in from as far away as Martin City.

By the fifties, with the development of Ruskin Heights and the new residential areas spreading south of Hickman Mills, the district emphasized grade schools. The first, named after long-time school board member C.A. Burke, was built between Hickman Mills and Ruskin on the west side of the railroad tracks. Soon to follow, Truman Elementary School on Bannister Road east of Blue Ridge accommodated students to the northeast. But the district was growing so fast that there was still concern about classroom space. Enrollment had jumped from 513 grade school students in 1951 to 2,806 in 1956. The brick high school was now the junior high and a newly constructed one story modern Ruskin High stood on the same grounds just to the east, across from the new Presbyterian church. This high school was built so that a second floor could be added as the need arose.

Roads were another problem. On the east side of the Kansas City Southern Line, the new shopping center, Ruskin Center, filled quickly with merchants like the Crown Drug, A&P and Ruskin Hardware. In the middle of the Center a large dime store, Ben Franklin, stocked everything from can openers to hair nets. Independent owner Sam Walton, just starting his career, was careful to supply the community's needs. Soon other merchants followed, making this the most complete shopping area for miles around. There was a dentist, fabric shop, toy store, bakery, barbershop, beauty shop, shoe store, dry cleaner's, jeweler, dance studio and public library. Convenient shopping brought people from all over the area. Traffic along Blue Ridge kept a pace undreamed of a few years before.

Ever since the days when Quantril's raiders hid out in area farms, the path that became Blue Ridge was well traveled. Early settlers along this high ridge saw the prairie rise and fall in long waves of natural grasses and wildflowers, and the sky majestically spread itself across the unbroken horizon like a mother with outstretched arms. It quickly became a commercial route, running from Grandview to Independence and crossing many roads leading into Kansas City. Now, with added commuter traffic, its narrow two lanes made for a true rush hour.

On the west side of Hickman Mills, U.S. Highway 71 provided the only other direct route north to Kansas City and south to Grandview and Richards-Gebaur Air Force Base. First known as Missouri State Highway 1, it became a U.S. highway as part of a large road improvement project instigated while Harry Truman was Jackson County Presiding Judge.

Both these roads had been paved during the thirties, when the community was small and rural. At that time trains still stopped at Grandview and Hickman Mills depots and the Missouri Pacific line accommodated residents in the Martin City area. Throughout the thirties and forties farms still surrounded these small towns. Life moved at a slow pace and centered around church and school activities. But, like the rest of post-war America, change was altering long established communities, bringing with it new problems and new visions.

Everyone talked of growth and progress. By the time the subdivision was finished, construction had started on another Ruskin grade school, this one named for William Johnson. Truman Corners, a larger shopping center going up next to the old Truman homestead north of Grandview, would add to the traffic problems. But already there was talk of a new four-lane Highway 71 which would hook up with the new interstate system. Even the landmarks changed. The new silver 1,600-ton water tower, rising behind Ruskin Center and just south of Burke Elementary School, could be seen for miles. More than the billboard along Blue Ridge, it identified the entrance to Ruskin Heights, and symbolized a fresh community looking toward the future.

This new generation of home owners shared a common optimism. They might worry about global destruction by the A-bomb, but basically they felt good about where they lived and their future. Connected by radio and especially television, they shared a new popular culture that affirmed optimism. Like rock and roll, still in its infancy in 1957, they caught the tempo of a nation pulsing with new energy. A rhythm of hope beat through bedroom communities like Ruskin Heights, creating a new accompaniment to the American Dream.

Our house was a Model "D" wihout the crawl space.

Our lot, Sweet Sue and me.
Old Ruskin High School (junior high) and water tower on the horizon.

"LOOK AT THIS CLOUD"

II

It was a windy Monday. Marjorie Langford was up before dawn preparing for Ruskin's junior/senior breakfast at Swope Park. As senior advisor, Marjorie's job was to make sure the event ran smoothly. She met principal Blaine Steck at the park and together they worked to keep plates and napkins from blowing off picnic tables. After breakfast, the seniors were scheduled to practice for graduation in the school gymnasium. Marjorie planned to spend the rest of the day finishing up end-of-the-school-year paperwork. Already she could tell it was going to be a long day.

At least it wasn't raining. The soggy weekend spoiled many picnics and ball games. The Crest Drive-In, in the heart of Hickman Mills on Highway 71, lost business. Anyone wanting to see Frank Sinatra in *The Man With The Golden Arm* and Randolph Scott in *Tall Man Riding* had missed their opportunity. The screen was now taken over by *Flying Leathernecks* and *Sea Devils*.

Richards-Gebaur's annual air show still drew a large crowd but some of the planned maneuvers were scrapped due to weather conditions. Two F-102 supersonic jets from Duluth demonstrated their skill over the crowd, producing an unearthly roar that added to the thrill of performance. It was a sound nearby residents of Martin City and Ruskin Heights were used to hearing from this flourishing Cold War air base.

It hadn't been a good weekend for real estate either. Gene Montee had sold his Ruskin house on 109th Street in exchange for a house in Olathe, and the buyer planned to sell the Ruskin house himself. The weekend brought no lookers so the Montees intended to move their possessions out over Memorial Day. There was no hurry: they weren't closing until the morning of the 20th.

It was laundry day. The morning *Times* predicted more rain for the evening, so housewives got busy hanging out the wash. It wouldn't take long to dry with all the wind. But Jean McCoy had a hard time keeping diapers from wrapping themselves around the clothesline and her good friend and neighbor, Mary Northcraft, kept chasing diapers that blew off the line. Helen Boyles and next door neighbor Betty Sturdevant, visited over the fence as they hung up laundry, and worried that even all the wind wouldn't dry things if it got much more humid.

At three-thirty, Joe Audsley arrived at work as radar operator for the National Severe Storm Forecast Center. He knew he was in for a busy night. He and his partner, Bob Babb, would have their hands full keeping up with all the developing weather. Audsley's radar system, a WSR57, was the state of the art and mounted on the tallest downtown building, 911 Grand. It was originally a Navy design for spotting aircraft. Although it was the best available, there were drawbacks for weather use. Naval radar was not concerned with ground clutter and this unit could be affected by ground clutter up to forty miles away. It also was not designed to see through supercell storm formations. Unknown to tornado researchers of the time, tornadoes frequently form at the back side of a super cell. But there was so much thunderstorm and tornadic activity in the area that Audsley and Babb were looking for tornadoes everywhere. There was activity not just in Kansas and western Missouri, but in southwestern Iowa and southeastern Nebraska as well. By the time most people were driving home from work, several tornadoes had been reported in northern Kansas and south-central Nebraska, and two tornadoes spotted near Maryville, Missouri. As families prayed over dinner, the NSSFC issued this report to radio and television stations all over the area:

"Radar at the Kansas City Weather Bureau shows this storm to be very severe and moving northeastward in the general direction of Kansas City at about 50 mph. ...For the present it appears that Kansas City may expect high winds accompanied by hail by eight o'clock this evening or shortly before."

When my dad sat down in his favorite living room chair next to the picture window that looked out over a southern sky, radio and television newsmen were telling of numerous unconfirmed reports of tornadoes in the vicinity of Paola and Ottawa, Kansas.

But my parents were not watching television or listening to the radio. They were reading in the *Kansas City Star* about a reduction of armaments and armed forces in a place few had heard of called Vietnam, and laughing over the cute little beagle in a new comic strip debuting in the *Times* that day called *Peanuts*. If they had turned on the television when they noticed the sky looked funny, they would have heard this ominous report:

"Pilot reports tornado on ground north of Grandview moving north-east. Appears to be headed toward the east edge of the city."

DARRYL HAYNES

I was riding in a car near Garnett, Kansas, and I saw this greenish-gray-looking cloud. It was turning violently, so we pulled the car over and watched. Tentacles were reaching down out of the cloud and bouncing off the ground. First, two or three came down and went back up into the cloud and then more came down, still dancing around. As the tornado developed, five and up to ten tentacles came down together and joined. We kept watching as they formed into a black shaft close to the ground. The next thing we saw was parts of a nearby filling station and motel flying up from the ground.

WALT BODINE

"Jake" (Henry L.) Jacobson, who was a public-service forecaster, called the WDAF newsroom, where I was a newscaster and said, "I'm looking at a very bad storm coming up the line. It's already past Emporia. I just think it would be a good idea to keep your staff in tonight. Don't send them out for dinner."

We had a fifteen-minute newscast at 6:00 and normally I did the Kansas City weather forecast at the end of the news. But in this case they moved me up to the front, as I remember, and I covered the coming storm as best I could.

We also did ten minutes of radio news at 5:45. We gave the weather with some degree of caution even at that time, but with no more information than we had you couldn't just say, "Here comes a big tornado." You'd terrify people. I kept thinking maybe Jake would call back and say, "OK, everything is clearing up, issue an all clear," but he didn't.

MARJORIE LANGFORD

When I got home I was pooped so I stretched out on the couch. My husband was teaching at the junior college in the city. Marvin Jr., who was eight, came in and aroused me and said, "Mother, they say there's a storm coming," and I didn't pay too much attention. Finally he got my attention and I realized there was a storm in the area. I gathered some things together and took him to the base-ment. I needed to hem my dress for graduation so I took it and a needle and thread with me.

STANLEY JEPPESEN

My wife and daughter and I were visiting my in-laws just west of Martin City. Her parents lived next door to her sister and brother-in-law, so there was a crowd of seventeen waiting out the storm. When warnings were first issued, my wife Bonnie's parents were at our house, and Bonnie, who was five months pregnant at the time, got nervous and wanted to go to her parent's house. I had run from the 1946 Martin City tornado and figured Martin City would be a safe place to go because a tornado wouldn't hit there twice. I got to Blue Ridge and Blue River Road and the sky was blue to the south. But when I got out of the car there at their house I could feel it. Something didn't feel right. This was about five or ten minutes before it hit.

I wouldn't sit down. I walked out, looked west, and saw that the clouds were tornadic. Besides the '46 tornado, I'd seen tornadoes in Nebraska when I was a boy, so I knew what I was seeing. The clouds were like boiling water, working their way across the sky and they were a terrible green color that you can't forget. One of my brothers-in-law said tornadoes just have a narrow path, that you'd have to be smack dab in the path to get hit, so he wasn't worried. Boy, within a couple of minutes I moved that guy.

I heard it coming. Everyone else thought I was nuts. They thought it was just the sound of a train because the tracks were nearby. I said, train hell. You smell it and feel it and at the same instance you hear it.

I stepped out around the house and saw that sucker. The funnel was on the southern side of the cloud and I had never seen such solid blackness in a cloud, never before or since.

I started hollering. Everyone was in the newer, smaller house, and I knew it would never withstand such a storm. Neither house had a basement, but the older house was more solid so everyone ran to it. Everyone except me. I grabbed my daughter, who was three, and headed for the railroad tracks because I knew if I could get to the tracks I could get in a culvert. I looked up and that funnel was probably one hundred feet away. I didn't make the culvert. I hit the ground with my Sheryl underneath me.

SHERYL JEPPESEN MCKINNEY

Dad really wanted to go to a storm cellar on 103rd Street, but

Mom wanted to go to Grandma and Grandpa's. My grandparents went ahead and took me in their car so my parents had to follow them.

I remember being at my uncle Bob and aunt Dee's house and a lot of people eating dinner. Some of Bob's family was there as well as Aunt Dee's, who is Mom's sister, so there were seventeen of us. I heard the word "funnel" and wondered what a funnel was. Then everyone got up from the table. There was a lot of commotion and maddening confusion as people started running across the driveway to the bigger house.

My mother went into the house but stood at the doorway because my dad was on the porch and wouldn't come in. I was between them. They started arguing back and forth, "I'll take Sheryl," "No, I'll take her." Here a funnel, whatever that was, was coming and the wind was getting strong and I heard what sounded like the biggest train in the world and I didn't know what was going on. It was terrible. Dad took me finally, but by that time we couldn't get any further than the garage.

CHARLIE COOK

My mother died on the 18th of May and her visitation was the evening of the 20th. Normally, I would have been at my store, Cook's Market, in Martin City all through that evening, but not this night. My butcher, Lowell Adkinson, was at the store and I knew he'd take care of things. He was in the process of buying the store from me so, he was an associate as well as a butcher.

We lived just north of Hickman Mills, and all the way to the funeral home I noticed the sky looked funny but I didn't think too much about it. I had more personal things on my mind.

NORMAN CARON

I was a Kansas City Police patrolman at the time and I covered 85th Street, State Line to Troost, from four PM to midnight. That was the city's southern border, but there were plans to annex the following year. Because of that, some Kansas City policemen were trained as deputy sherrifs by the county so they would know the area. A buddy of mine, who was one of these duputies, was out south and heard on his police radio that a tornado was on the ground near Olathe. There was only one radio frequency then, so we all heard what was going on. The dispatcher told us to stay put in our own districts until further notice so they'd know where to find us if we were needed. We followed the development of that tornado very closely.

CLYDE RENKEN

I was working at Bendix and it was payday. That night after supper we went over to Raytown to a Katz store there where I could cash my check and we could get a few things. We got home just about seven-thirty and turned on the TV. You could kind of feel it in the air that something wasn't exactly right. The TV was rambling on about one thing and another, then all of a sudden they said there was a tornado on the ground at Spring Hill, Kansas headed toward Olathe. They hadn't much more than said that than the electricity went off. We went outside to see what was happening, to tell if it was headed our way and to see what we could do. The people next door were gone, but their two boys were there with a babysitter. My wife went over and got them because they didn't have a basement and we did.

Another neighbor was out looking at the sky too. He didn't have a basement, so I told him to get his wife and come down to ours, just in case, but he said he'd be fine at home.

Just about that time, here came this big black blob, that's all I can tell you, it was dragging on the ground. I turned to the neighbor and said, "Well, I can't take time to argue with you," and I went down, too.

JIM AND AGGIE TURNBAUGH

Aggie: I was supposed to go to a Jaycee Mates meeting at the Ruskin Shopping Center but when the tornado warnings were issued we called it off. Growing up I had seen tornadoes and knew very well what they were capable of doing. We lived in Grandview at the time, and Jim and our neighbors were outside the back door looking west for it. They found it. They were so fascinated by it that I couldn't get them to move. Only my dog and I went to the basement.

Jim: It looked like it was coming right for us from Martin City. The thing was so huge we were sure it was going to swing right down Main Street, which was where our office, the *Jackson County Advocate,* was. As a newspaperman I just couldn't turn away from witnessing this horrible storm that I was sure would effect our community. It's a good thing for me that it passed to the northeast of us.

WILLIS AND MAXINE WATKINS

Willis: We were eating dinner and had the TV on. A report came on that a tornado was spotted on the ground in Ottawa, Kansas and moving in a northeast direction. That was the only alert we got because the power went off shortly after that. We were still eating so we pulled out some candles— the kids thought that was great— and I went to the front door to check the sky. In the west southwest it was dark, but due south was clear. It looked like everything was going to go north of us. We talked about where we would go if a tornado came and decided the crawl space would be the best place.

Maxine: I remembered a neighbor across the street whose husband was out of town. I thought I'd go over and ask her if she needed candles. I stepped out on the front porch and there was this humongous big squiggle.

Willis: The only flashlight we had was in the car, so I decided to get that. I told Maxine I was going to get it and told her to get the kids. It was about a half mile away. It didn't look like tornadoes I had seen pictures of. It was really bearing down on us at that point. The clouds were hanging low and then there was just this big short column coming down. I could see stuff boiling around the bottom of it. Because we had just talked about it, there was no hesitation about what to do.

When I saw that twister I did some silly things. First I got the flashlight out of the car. Then I came back into the dining area where there were double windows. I'd always heard you're suppose to open windows to equalize the pressure so I opened them. There was a big buffet in front of these windows, and on top a delicate coffee carafe. I was afraid the wind might blow that carafe off the buffet so I laid it on the floor. Of course we never saw that carafe again.

PETE AND DOROTHY KOTSIFAKIS

Dorothy : We didn't expect it. We thought it was something we could sit out. I was talking to my next door neighbor, Anna Lee, whose husband and daughter were at the A&P store, and we decided to go to the basement to play cards because it looked like it was going to storm.

At that time Bendix, where Pete worked, was putting out all this information about how to prepare for an atomic attack, how to have block captains with food stored at that house in case of attack. My daughter was watching *I Love Lucy* and Pete was mowing the backyard. We had only been in the house for a few months, and it wasn't even quite finished. Our daughter came in and said she heard on TV to go to the basement, to the southwest corner. Then the electricity went off. So we decided to pick up the kids and all go to the basement to practice an atomic-attack drill. We took water and the dog.

Anna Lee didn't come, so I made sure the front door was unlocked so she could come on in to play cards. I came upstairs and looked out the picture window for her and here was her car going *zoom* down the street. Her husband and daughter had come back from A&P and they saw the tornado coming. We could see that big black cloud back there bouncing up and down.

Pete: Looking out the basement window I could see it coming. It looked like a big curtain coming down with sparks in it and I saw some trash cans and things rolling in front of it. I looked at our trees when it got close and they were all pointing northeast. One of the reasons we bought this house was because of all the beautiful trees on the property.

JUDY JONES HECKADON

My mother and grandmother were ironing and my dad was downtown at a meeting. Mom heard it before she saw anything, but she thought it was a train because there was a track a couple blocks away. When it got louder and louder she realized what it was and yelled for us to go to the basement. Grandma and my sister made it but, because I was four, she decided to carry me, so we were behind the others.

ELINOR STEINBRUECK

It looked like it was going to storm. I was outside at a neighbor's yard with my two little girls while my husband was at work. I told my neighbor I was going to go home and put my windows down. While I was in the house my mother called and said there was a storm coming, but she didn't call it a tornado. I went back to the neighbor's and she suggested I stay there until the storm subsided.

Her husband was reading a magazine and we couldn't get him to the door to look out. Pretty soon we saw it coming. He said, "Let's get out of here!" So instead of going to the basement we got into their car. We were just lucky because of the way we turned. If we had turned the other way we would have hit the water tower.

DONNA BRAMBLE WILLIAMS

Dad was at work and Mom, my nine-year-old brother Jay, and I were watching *I Love Lucy*. I was about half finished pin-curling my hair when our neighbor, Dick Davis, called and said to come over to their house. We had a half basement but they had a full basement, so we left. I was in the eighth grade and did a lot of babysitting for the two Davis girls. Corky— Mrs. Davis— was like a big sister to me, so it was only natural we would wait the storm out together.

The more we heard about the tornado the more Dick thought we should get out of there. So we all piled into their 1955 Chevy and took off toward Burke Elementary School, but for some reason Dick changed his mind and turned around back south.

GEORGE MOORE

I was at the Crest Food Center on Hickman Mills Drive when the tornado hit. The pharmacist was busy with a customer and the phone rang, so he asked me to answer it. It was somebody calling to tell us to look out the back door at the storm coming. There was a big iron security door and it took me a minute to get it open. The tornado was coming right toward us from the southwest. I looked right straight up at it.

GENE AND MARJORIE MONTEE

Gene: We had just sold our house and signed the papers that morning. Technically the house wasn't ours that night, but all our belongings were still in it.

Marjorie: The boys and I were sick. We had gone to the doctor in Grandview and were on our way home when we decided to stop at the drugstore in Hickman Mills to have the prescription filled. We stayed in the car while my husband went in to get the medicine. Our sons were five and six and they had never seen hail before, so we were talking about the hail that began to fall. And then it stopped. There was no wind, just dead stillness. Gene came to the front door of the drugstore and said to get in there quick. I had never seen that expression on his face before. The pharmacist had gotten a call while Gene was in there, and they all looked out the back door to see it coming right at us.

When we got into the store Gene didn't say a word to me but took us over to the greeting card section. We got on the floor and laid over our kids. Our son Mark is deaf and couldn't understand what was going on, but everything was happening so quickly that we didn't have a chance to communicate to him what was happening.

CHARLES GRAY

I was on vacation that week from my job as news director for WHB radio, and using the time to do a little free-lance work at Calvin recording studios. I was down there that evening and as soon as the reports of a tornado on the ground came in, we disbanded the crew. I ran a one-man news department at WHB and had a phone in my car, so I stopped to get my wife and headed for the scene. All the way out there we listened to Walt Bodine give updates on WDAF radio. It was Walt's broadcasts that told me where I should be going.

MIKE ANGOTTI

I owned the Ruskin Hardware store and I happened to be working up there that night. The guy I had working for me and I went outside to check the sky about 7:30. We sat on a car bumper there in front of my store and watched a huge cloud move our way. About then my wife called. She wanted me to come get her and our five kids and bring them all back to the store. We didn't have a basement at home. Of course we didn't have one at the store either, but she wanted us all to be together. We talked about where we would go in the store if it turned out to be a tornado and decided the back, where the big nail bins were, would be the safest place. We never made it.

SIDNEY BATES

I was fourteen at the time and attending a Boy Scout meeting at Burke Elementary School. During the meeting a lot of the parents kept coming in and picking up their sons. I couldn't figure out why, but then someone told us there was a tornado coming our way. My dad was one of the leaders and, since not all of the boys left, we stayed there.

Counting leaders and boys there were about twelve of us that stayed. We went outside and watched the funnel. It was so big we could see it for a long time and we could tell it was coming right at us. Someone yelled to get into the basement, but Burke didn't have a basement, so we went back into the school and laid down on the floor in the hallway where there were no windows.

BLAINE STECK
   I didn't really know there was a tornado coming until it hit the school building. It was the night between baccalaureate and graduation. I went up there for two reasons: to meet with the president of the school board, to see about giving out diplomas, and I had an appointment with the school nurse. I met the president at seven o'clock and I was to meet the nurse at seven-forty. I had no indication whatsoever of the weather being bad, but somehow I knew what it was when I heard the noise.

AUDREY GERRED BECKLEY
   My husband, Glen, was president of the school board and he was up at the high school at a meeting with Blaine Steck. He was going to announce the names of the graduates the next night and wanted to make sure he knew how to pronounce all their names. We had four daughters. They were all doing homework or playing around the house and I was sprinkling clothes. I was waiting for my next door neighbor, who was going to drive me up to the Ruskin Center's fabric shop, because I planned to cut out a dress that night for one of my daughters. She came over to tell me her husband, who was a TWA pilot, said the weather was too bad to go anywhere. Well, I said I wasn't going to let any old storm stop me, but we didn't go.
   About that time, her husband, Art Kelly, came over and told me in no uncertain terms to grab the kids and go to the basement in the house on the other side of his. I said I wasn't going to leave my husband, because he wasn't back from the high school yet, but I rounded up the girls. As I was leaving our house, I saw my husband running down the street. Fortunately, we lived just four houses from the school. He had finished his meeting with Blaine, stepped outside and saw how bad the sky looked. He was right behind me as we ran to the basement and just before we went down, we turned around to look. We saw the high school go.

HELEN BOYLES
   My husband, Skeeter, and Art Kelly, who lived across the street, were sitting at the dining room table talking about Art buying our

'56 Chevy. Another neighbor called and said she heard on the radio there was a tornado around Stanley, Kansas, headed our way. Art went home.

Our daughter, Libby, who was in the third grade, heard and told us what to do with our important papers and to open windows and doors. She told us to be sure and take a flashlight and coat. She went to two or three neighbors and told them what to do too. I went along with her. The neighbors took her seriously because she was so upset and had been studying tornadoes in school.

RUSS MILLIN

I was at my Monday night Optimist Club meeting which was always held at a restaurant on Highway 71 called Chicken Cuisine. We had just started the meeting when someone came in and told us there was a report of a tornado so we all went outside. We could see it coming, a long black column moving across the horizon. We turned on a radio and heard the tornado was headed for Holmes Park, which was north of us, but everyone wanted to go home anyway. We just canceled the meeting. We never thought it was near Ruskin Heights, but when I got there it had already hit. I drove as far as I could, but I didn't get very far.

JANIE KILLION

I was in the basement of the Baptist church babysitting sixteen little children while their parents were at a dinner upstairs. About fifteen minutes before the tornado hit, I walked a couple blocks away to the A&P at Ruskin Center to get some crackers for the kids. While I was in the store it started to rain and I thought I should just wait there until it stopped. The raindrops were very big and I thought we were in for a good rain. But it didn't start raining harder so I thought I better get back over to the kids, so I left.

JEANNE JOHNSTON GORMAN

I worked in the payroll department of the IRS. I never worked late but some people were being laid off so I was trying to get their checks ready. We only had one car so my husband was supposed to pick me up. Well, it started raining hard and the lights went out. We knew something was happening because it was so bad out, but of course we didn't have a radio. There were probably only five of us working in the building at the time. A friend of my husband's said he'd take me home because of the storm.

ERNESTINE PETERSON

We were sitting at the table eating. The phone rang and my sister said, "You better look out. There's a tornado coming your way," so I said, "OK, I'll look." She called back a couple of minutes later and said, "You didn't seem real impressed with this storm. You better look again." So I walked out on the front step and I could see it coming.

Quite a few of the neighbors were coming too, because we were the only house on this end of the block with a basement. There was a woman who lived behind us whose husband was in Korea. She had two teenage sons and a younger boy about seven. I told her to come on over. I lifted the little boy over the fence and they all ran to the basement. The two older boys watched the basement steps and helped people down and made sure the little kids stayed down there. We ended up with twenty-five people in the basement.

BETTY HAMBEL

Like everyone else, you think it's not going to hit you. When I looked out the back door and saw it swinging down the backyard, that's when I knew we were going to be smashed. I saw it as it hit the high school. The thing was just swinging back and forth.

We had the TV on, we had plenty of warning, but, you know, you keep walking out and looking, watching the sky. I asked the guy across the street what he thought and he said he thought it was going to blow. The sky had a yellow cast and you could have cut the air with a knife.

We were so new we didn't really know many people. We found out later there was one basement on the block. If we had asked about that basement when the news people first told us to go, we would have been safe. That's all that was on TV, instructions about what to do. We just figured these were things that happened to other people.

THELMA KIRKMAN

We both worked at that time. We'd come home and I had fixed us a bite to eat and we were ready to sit down. My husband's cousin called us and said there was a storm coming through. Roy went out the back and didn't see anything, so he went out front and bricks were blowing off Ruskin High School just to our east. It was pulling the bricks right off.

We were real friendly with the people next door. In fact, Roy worked with the man. Roy went by their door and said, "Jim, get Marylou and the babies and get on the floor. The tornado is here on us." So he came back into our house, grabbed me, and I just hung up the phone telling our cousin, "Goodbye, this is it."

AL CAUDLE

I was at a scout meeting in the basement of the Presbyterian church. I was a Boy Scout leader then, and this was our regular meeting. One of the boys had a transistor radio, and about ten minutes before the tornado hit he came up to the other leader and said he just heard Martin City had been hit. I went upstairs to look out the front door. These were very large glass-front doors, and I could see a huge black cloud that looked like a shaft. There was a meeting upstairs, so I warned them to come to the basement.

REV. HARRY DALE COLLIER

During the day Florence Miller, the church secretary, and I worked on the church newsletter. I had been the pastor of the Ruskin Presbyterian Church since it opened in 1954. I headed up the second column of page one with "It's Later Than You Think." Then the stencils for the newsletter were completed and laid aside to be run off the next day.

By seven o'clock I had returned to the church for a meeting. My family was home in the church manse. The callers meeting was being held in the sanctuary and the Boy Scouts were meeting directly below in the Fellowship Hall.

As I remember it, our meeting was underway when Al Caudle came up from the basement telling us about bad weather and a possible tornado. He said that we should come to the basement. I must confess that I went reluctantly. As I passed under the laminated beams of the sanctuary, I did not believe that anything could disturb them.

As I approached the narthex area, I saw people streaming into the church, going down the steps into the basement, and Fellowship Hall was filling up with men, women and children.

DIANE NEHRING LEVALLEY

My five-year-old sister and I were watching *I Love Lucy* and they announced there was a tornado coming. I was ten and kind of knew what a tornado was, but I didn't have an impression that it was something to worry about. My dad was downtown so Mom told us to get in the car. We had only lived in Ruskin for a couple months, but Mom had become good friends with a neighbor. Her husband was at work too, so she and her two kids joined us. We were all in the car, ready to go to the Presbyterian church basement, when Mom decided to go back into the house and open the windows. We only had to go about a half a block but the tornado was right behind us. As soon as we got out of the car I could feel the wind pushing at my back. Then my mother yelled, "Run for your life!"

DEAN EVANS

There had been a jail break at the Jackson County Jail the day before and the escapees had taken some guns with them and thrown them into a field. As a reporter for the *Kansas City Star*, I was sent to follow police academy cadets as they searched for the guns. Well, the field we looked in was covered with poison ivy. I was so badly covered that I stopped on the way home and bought a new pair of jeans. I was so anxious to get those contaminated jeans off that when the keys stuck a little bit as I was taking them out of the ignition, I jerked them out, leaving the ignition on. This was a '54 Chevy and you could do that. I took a bath as soon as I got home and put the new jeans on, but because they were new I didn't have my car keys and billfold in the pockets.

Later, my wife and I were out in the front yard watching this big greenish-black cloud and talking about how Kansas City must be getting quite a storm. Our next door neighbor was there too, and our three-year-old daughter, who didn't want to go to bed until she saw the storm. Our neighbor happened to look to the southwest and suddenly said, "Oh my God!" I turned around and looked and there was this tornado. The edge of that cloud was right over our heads. I yelled, "Get in the car!" I didn't have to go inside to get my wife or daughter or my car keys. Because the ignition was open we jumped in and took off. I left tire marks on the garage floor and the street.

TREVA WOODLING

After we ate dinner I told Harry, my husband, I was going up to the shopping center to Ben Franklin to get little gifts for the shower I was giving my sister the next night. I had everything else done but that. I was shopping around up there, picking up little party favors, and all of a sudden the lights went out. I thought, Gee, it must be going to storm. I went up front to pay and at the checkouts they were lighting candles. No one knew anything about a tornado. They couldn't get their cash registers to open because their power was off and a couple in front of me were waiting because they didn't have the correct change. I added mine up in my head and asked if I could pay and go because I had the right amount.

When I got home Harry said, "My God, where have you been? Don't you know there's a tornado heading this way?" The whole sky was lit up with a weird orangish-yellow glow. I looked to the southwest corner and there was a huge cloud coming. There was no funnel, just a giant cloud on the ground. To see it, you'd think it was going to wipe out all of Ruskin Heights.

I asked Harry why he didn't take the kids and go someplace and he said he didn't want to leave without me. There weren't any basements on our street, but the Presbyterian church was just a few houses away. We should have started running to the church basement right then. But instead, Harry changed his pants to the ones that had his car keys and wallet and I put raincoats on our three kids. Then Harry yelled to get into the car. When we stepped outside, something just told me to go back into the house and lay on the floor, but Harry and the kids were already in the car.

When we got in front of the church I yelled, "church basement!" because it was the only thing I could think of. He drove across the church lawn to get to the front door. We got about halfway across the church lawn and a little girl ran in front of the car. We had to stop or we would have hit her. We got out of the car, but by that time debris was already flying.

HERB GREEN
I had been out in the yard painting a redwood fence when my wife Edna came out and said she heard on the TV there was a tornado coming. The sky had been kind of green for a while and it gave you an eerie feeling. We had a brand new car, so we went over to get our neighbors and then we left. We got out just as it was coming up the hill at the high school. We went to the left toward Blue Ridge and the tornado went to the right.

JOE KRAMER

I was home with my wife and three little boys when I got a call from work to come in and help out. I was working at KCMO in the newsroom, primarily for radio at that time. They were having a hard time doing their regular amount of evening news, plus handling, processing and putting on the air all the weather bulletins. So they asked if I would come back down to work and help out. I left Ruskin and drove to 31st and Grand, where the station was at that time. It was dusky, like a storm was brewing, but it didn't seem that bad.

I walked into the newsroom all ready to sit down and process weather bulletins, but someone told me I should go back where I'd come from because a major tornado had just struck Ruskin.

I left my personal car at the radio station and took a station news car that had a two-way radio and was identified by exterior markings, which was a fortunate thing.

LEON FELSON

I was acting administrator of Menorah Hospital, and that night I was at a meeting in the library, sitting with four doctors and two other administrative personnel. We had received several calls from physicians who were suppose to attend, [saying that they] were going to be late or had decided not to attend because of inclement weather.

Riding over to the hospital at seven o'clock I had heard some reports of unsettled weather conditions and that there was a possibility of tornadoes in the area. But unsettled weather in the spring in Kansas City had been rather standard, and I gave it no further thought.

JEAN HENDERSHOT

I had gone downtown about six-thirty to the Municipal Auditorium with my friends Jim and Doris. Jim was playing piano in the band at an industrial show. They had lots of displays, including one from the fire department.

As we left Ruskin and drove downtown, my friends mentioned we might have storms and I just laughed because the sky was clear and the sun was out. I said, "If we're going to have a storm I don't know where it's going to come from."

Jim started playing at seven-thirty. Doris and I walked around. Soon there was an announcement on the public-address system for all firemen to leave the auditorium and go to Ruskin Heights, that there had been a tornado. Even then that didn't disturb me a whole lot because I always thought of tornadoes dipping down, taking out a house or two and going back up. It wasn't too much after that they announced again for anybody who had a van or something that could transport people to go out to Ruskin. Jim didn't even say goodbye to the band. He just got up from the piano bench and said to us, "We're going home."

STEVE GALLER

We were all outside that evening. I was playing with my younger brother and sister and my dad was digging weeds. Mom was sitting on the front patio and she was the first to notice that Brownie, our dog, was acting funny. He kept running to the end of the driveway, then he'd cock his head and sniff the air, then run back to Mom and whine. Mom told him to go away, but he started biting the hem of her dress, and then he'd repeat the whole process again. Finally we looked at the sky and Mom told me to go turn on the TV. At that point, they were announcing there was a tornado on the ground in Martin City, headed for Ruskin.

Dad started throwing all the garden tools and bikes into the garage, but he was in such a hurry that he didn't leave enough room for the car, so he could only get the car into the garage part way. By this time there were other neighbors outside yelling, "Tornado coming!" and everyone was running to the corner house where there was a basement. We joined them with Brownie leading the way.

PEGGY MCNAMARA

Mom and my younger brother, Mike, had just got back from the A&P store to get a special treat for Mike's kindergarten class because graduation was the next day. I was watching *I Love Lucy* when a weather bulletin broke in. We all started getting ready to go to the basement on the corner. Mom was dressing my baby sister, Shannon, and telling me to get my shoes on, there was a tornado coming. I said, "What the heck is a tornado?" and didn't pay much attention. I was only eight. Dad was gathering up raincoats and told us to hurry and run for the corner, he'd be right behind us. I never did get my shoes on.

JEAN HAYES

After dinner we went to my husband Vernie's sister's house. We were watching television there and they stopped the show for a weather bulletin saying to watch for high winds and torrential rains. We decided we better head on home because we had left the windows open.

We got to about 87th and Blue Ridge and I noticed the sun looked weird, kind of eerie, dust covered, and an odd color, not sun colored, but there was no evidence of anything more at that time.

When we got home I turned on the A's game and went outside. A little bit later I went back into the house to get a bottle for Becky, who was a year old at the time, and then I heard on the radio there was a tornado on the ground two miles south of Grandview.

I went back outside to tell my husband and we noticed people looking at the sky. Vernie started yelling to people to go to the Miller's house on the corner because they had a basement.

MYRNA SMITH
We had plenty of warning, but I didn't realize it was really coming until I saw it hit the high school, which was just up the street. We had both the radio and television on and everyone was out watching the sky, but we didn't know quite what to make of it all.

PAUL AND JANE POTTER
Paul: The weather did seem strange that day. It was windy and balmy and cloudy. While I was waiting for my ride to work, about three o'clock that afternoon, I said to Jane, "Boy, somebody's going to get a real bad storm tonight." We could tell by the way the air was pumping.

Jane: I didn't have the TV or radio on. I didn't know anything about it. My mom called me and said, "Jane, get out of the house, there's a storm coming your way," so I dropped everything, grabbed Pam, who was three, and went next door to the Miller's basement.

Paul: I took my lunch break at Bendix about seven-thirty and that night I was listening to the A's game on the radio when they announced all the severe weather. The guy I rode with and I were trying to decide whether to go home or not, but we decided to give it another hour. We figured they would announce anything over the intercom if things got really bad. They did make an announcement, after it hit Ruskin. I left work on an hour's pass and got back to work three days later.

JEAN FROUNFELTER

I was giving the baby her evening bottle and we were trying to catch *I Love Lucy* but we couldn't get much of Lucy for all the warnings that were on the air. They were telling us all the things we should do, like turn off water and electricity and to leave windows open. Then they said, "A plane flying over Grandview has now sighted a tornado going over Grandview moving in a northeast direction." I said, "Ok girls," — we have four — "it's time to get our coats on and go to the neighbor's basement." So we did.

E.J. didn't hurry. He stayed behind and turned off the electricity and water, all those things. I was across the street looking west and I could see the darn thing with chunks moving in its tail. It must have been at the shopping center right then. I yelled to E.J., "Come on! It's coming down the street!" Nothing else was making any sound at all. It was that absolute silence before something happens. E.J. came out putting on his raincoat, looked west and ran as fast as he could over to the basement. He never ever hurries.

CLYDE OFNER JR.

I was at a filling station north of Ruskin, on Blue Ridge, with an uncle of mine from California, gassing up. He, his wife and three kids were visiting us and they were at my home with my wife and two boys. We stood there for a few minutes watching the funnel, then realized it was coming right toward us. By going in the opposite direction we managed to outrun it, but the wind took the paint right off the car. When we looked back toward the service station, everything was one color of gray. We couldn't distinguish one thing from another, but the station was gone.

JEAN MCCOY

My mother always said if you listen closely you can hear the wind in clouds. If a storm roars, it has a lot of wind in it.

We knew we were in the path about five minutes before it hit. Bob had just been to the shopping center to pick up some bookkeeping work. When he got home he kicked off his shoes, turned on the A's game and sat down at his desk to do some work.

I knew we were in for a storm, and I noticed the neighbors behind us picking up toys out in their yard, but I didn't think much of it. I put our baby, who was five months old, to bed and then started cleaning up the dishes. We never heard any warnings on the radio.

As I did the dishes I kept hearing the roar and I called out to Bob, "You better come look at this cloud." He looked out and saw it hit the Presbyterian church. He told me to get the baby and get under the bed. We got the baby under, and our heads, but that's about all.

DOLORES SCHUENEMEYER

I had just finished giving my kids a bath when I heard on TV that a tornado was headed our way. My husband and other men in the neighborhood were out in the front yard watching the sky and they kind of hee-hawed me and the other wives for being scared, but I wanted my husband to come help me get the kids to the basement. About that time the phone started ringing. My brother in Lee's Summit called to make sure we were keeping an eye on the weather and our friends, the Grosses there in Ruskin, called too, asking if they could come to our basement. Shirley was very pregnant , so I urged her to come right away. We had ordered new living room furniture and had all our old furniture in the basement, so we cleared a wall for everyone and I brought down a pot of coffee and a deck of cards so we could play bridge. My husband and Gordon were both flyers and they wanted to stay out studying the sky, but by the time we heard on the radio that a tornado was on the ground near Grandview, they could feel the pressure of the air changing and they joined us in the basement.

GORDON AND SHIRLEY GROSS

Shirley: We had a neighbor who was a Raytown policeman and he came over and told us he heard on his radio that a tornado had just hit Spring Hill, Kansas. This was the first clue we had that the weather was bad. We had been getting our kids ready for bed and didn't have a radio or TV on.

Gordon: I had flown a small plane in the area and had a mental map of how Ruskin lay in relationship to Spring Hill. I knew it was a straight line. In fact the line from Spring Hill, Kansas, to Sibley, Missouri, is as straight as a violin string.

We had no basement, so I said to Shirley, who was eight and a half months pregnant, "Get the kids and let's get going now." We went to our good friends the Schuenemeyers, who lived on the street just east of the Presbyterian church.

BILL MARTIN

We had just bought a new car. We were going on vacation and had decided to leave early, so we took the car back to the dealer to have it checked out. They gave us a loaner car.

My friend Will Witty and I were building a boat in his basement that evening. I went up to the Ruskin Hardware store to buy brass screws. I had the radio on in this loaner car when I came out of the hardware store. The wind was really kicking up, that's the first I knew we were in for serious weather. When I got up by the Presbyterian church the news cut in on the radio that a tornado was hitting Ruskin Heights. Of course I sped up immediately. The tornado was right behind me. The last thing I remember seeing, looking back toward the church, was the church actually being hit. I saw two cars swirling around above the church, and a ball of fire when it hit power lines. I dashed on down the street.

When I got to Witty's the whole family was out there yelling to come on in quick. I drove up the driveway and jumped out and we all dived down into their basement. I fell, tripping over their ten year old son, going down those basement steps. Just as we got down there in the basement, the tornado hit. I've often thought how lucky I was that the man who waited on me in the hardware store didn't take more time. I've always been grateful for his speedy service.

That car was completely ruined. Power lines swinging around wrapped themselves around the car. A two-by-four was driven into it and there was wood in the dashboard. It was torn all to pieces. Thank goodness it was a loaner.

GLEN AND JEAN WILLIAMS

Glen: I was on my last week of vacation. We just got back the day before from my in-laws and we brought back my wife's grandfather's piano. It was just beautiful. We were so proud of it. I remember walking by and looking at it, not dreaming that in a couple of hours it wouldn't be there.

I worked out in the yard all that day, mowing and planting trees, so I remember it was hard to breathe. The air seemed heavy.
Jean: I remember it was so humid and windy. All day it felt like the wind was whipping up a storm. I worked that day —I was a nurse at Menorah Hospital— and I heard the storm reports on the radio coming home, but we heard so many you just grew kind of immune to them after awhile. I stopped to get groceries at the A&P and when

I got home Glen was listening to a Cardinals baseball game on a St. Joseph radio station. They didn't say anything about storms but the station was staticy. It seemed to be getting dark quickly and looking like it was going to storm real hard so we closed the windows. Our son noticed great big raindrops on the front step. We all kind of gathered in the kitchen by the door going out into the garage. We had a basement but we didn't go to it.

We just huddled together in the kitchen. I actually didn't know that a tornado was coming. I just thought we were going to have a bad storm.

BILL MCCARTY

I was listening to the A's game on the radio and had no idea there was a tornado coming. Our neighbor behind us, who was an Air Force captain, called and wanted to know if his family could borrow our basement. I asked him why, and he said Richards-Gebaur had called him and said a tornado was headed this way.

I didn't notice the sky until then. Clouds were all to the north and it was clear to the south. That tornado just came down the path of the clouds. It must have been at the tail end of the storm.

While I was watching the sky, people started coming over. About the same time the captain arrived at our back door, so did twenty-five others.

AUSTIN SHUTE

I had stomach flu. My son, Michael, kept coming in and waking me up and saying, "Dad, there's a tornado coming," and I said, "Don't bother me with tornadoes." I'm from Massachusetts, and I had never given much thought to tornadoes. He finally got me to get out of bed and the damn thing was coming right toward us. The two kids and my wife following me, we ran two houses away to a basement. By that time it was almost on us.

Ruskin Heights before the storm, Summer 1954

LIKE A THOUSAND JETS

III

Would it hit? Would the tornado bear down and throw them into chaos? Or, at the last second, would it veer off in another direction, or hoist itself back into the clouds? There was little time to prepare, less time to think, but everyone tasted fear. There was the unmistakable shudder of disbelief. Selfishly, ravenously, it claimed everything in its way, demanding residency.

My father looked up from his paper and saw a greenish-yellow sky through the living room picture window. He went to the front door and there it was, a sickening black swirled mass heaving up chunks of the high school and Presbyterian church, a block and a half away. As it thundered toward us, Dad yelled at Mom to get my brother and me out of bed while he got the car ready. As soon as the words were out of his mouth he knew it was too late. They would have to find safety in the house. On his way back to help get us up, he heard a neighbor, Myrna Smith, screaming for her husband and baby daughter, who had run out of their house in the opposite direction from her. Dad pulled her and her young son into our house and made them lie down in the hallway with our family.

In the confusion, I walked out to the front window. When my mother told me to go to the hallway, I kept going, sleepy-stumbling back to bed. Because the other children were shielded by blankets and huddled under adults, my mother thought my dad had me, and my dad thought my mom had me.

Time ran out, sucked into the vortex along with everything else. As I slept through those last seconds of peace, a community held its breath.

BOB BABB

We had a constant flow of tornado reports from ground observers. In fact, we received so many we weren't able to put them all on the media circuit. Some were already outdated by the time we could get them out on the airways. I was talking to a telephone operator who called in with a tornado report, and while we were in the midst of the conversation the line went dead.

RUTH RAY

My husband was at work, so my three children and I left our home in Martin City with a neighbor and headed for the Methodist church in the center of Martin City. We could hear it coming and then, looking out the basement windows, I saw telephone poles flying through the air like toothpicks. There was an awful lot of trash flying around too. The worst part was hearing that great old church's foundation creak.

STANLEY JEPPESEN

The tornado was wide and short and the ground shook. Coming across the Kansas line straight at us, it was hitting nothing but timber. It rolled me and I saw the current coming around the smaller house as it exploded. Walls just bowed and then disappeared, where a few minutes before ten people had stood. Thank God they made it to the bigger house and had time to stand in the middle with a mattress over them. A tree hit that house and walls were knocked down and scattered, but it didn't explode. I felt like I was the size of a bug and someone was mowing grass over me. That's the effect it has.

I couldn't hold on to my daughter. I don't know if she moved or I moved. I couldn't comprehend, but I couldn't do it. Something was pulling her away.

A Studebaker hit me. It was scooting on its back bumper and I got hooked up in it and then it took off bouncing on the ground. That's what broke my leg. There were a lot of cars out in front of those two houses and I saw two of them fly over me.

Because of a bad car wreck the year before I had false teeth, and the inside of my mouth was raw from trying to hold on to my teeth. It blew my shoes off too. But I was never knocked out.

I remember it fading away and then dead silence. That's where the shock comes in. I didn't know where Sheryl was, or how Bonnie and her family were. You're sitting there and then in an instant everything's gone. You cannot explain the power.

MARJORIE AND GENE MONTEE

Marjorie: Mark, because he's deaf, kept raising his head, trying to figure out what was happening, and I kept pushing the poor baby's head back down on the floor. All of a sudden we started feeling boxes there in the store hitting us. All I could say was, "Jesus, Mary and Joseph." I thought I was saying it in a normal voice, but my husband and other son said I was screaming it.

Gene: The tornado lifted us and dropped us. We were laying there feeling this. We were on the edge of the funnel and it wasn't enough to pick us up and throw us, but it was just enough to tease us.

CLYDE RENKEN

My wife, two neighbor boys, their babysitter and Mrs. Gish, another neighbor, were already in the basement when I got down there. I shut the door and right away I could hear the first gravel hitting our house. It was only two minutes before the tornado was churning around and around. It sounded like there was a big meat grinder up there grinding up everything. The house just exploded. We had a brick chimney that broke off in three pieces and that fell on the flooring above us. We didn't know what it was, we just heard three big thumps. The windows broke and debris was everywhere. Glass was all over our hair. A two-by-four, eight feet long, sailed right through the wall like an arrow. My wife had been standing at that spot just a few moments before. When we rebuilt the house we left that board in the wall. It's still there.

Robert Jackson, General Manager of Debacker Chevrolet, found himself locked out of the car lot's basement as the tornado hit the car dealership at 117th and Highway 71 (now Hickman Mills Drive). He described his ordeal for the science journal "Weatherwise":

ROBERT JACKSON

(When the tornado was) about 150 feet away, I saw it pick up several cars and throw them thirty to forty feet in the air, one of them sailing along with the wind around outside of the funnel. The tornado came on across the street and our building began to fly apart before my eyes. A house to my right lifted off its foundation in one piece, then disintegrated, and wood flew everywhere.

I saw this terrible thing coming; it was very black just like mud. It had water, and mud and everything in it and it started slapping me on both sides and banging me behind this tree and at one time my feet would be almost straight up in the air as I held on to a tree, and another time it would bang me right in to the ground.

Then the blackness disappeared, the wind decreased to a near calm, and it became light. I thought the tornado had actually gone over, so I stood up and looked around. I felt that I was about to be picked up into the storm, but at the same time I felt "heavy." I realized I was looking up into the core of the tornado. I can't describe it, it was the most awesome thing. This column just mounted right straight into the heavens. It was bent toward the northeast up to about 200 to 300 feet, then straightened out and went straight up. I couldn't see anything whirling at all. I don't know how long I was inside the tornado, but I quickly lay down again and grabbed hold of the roots.

Then the back half hit me and it was black and smudgy again, dirt whipping through the air, automobiles hitting up and down. I remember that my shoes were about to come off my feet and I kept working my feet because I didn't want to lose my shoes for some crazy reason. I watched the tornado hit the Ruskin water tower dead center, but the tower didn't fall. Then a second wind hit me. I could hardly stand up against it, but it lasted only a few seconds, then it was calm.

I was filth from head to foot; it took me three baths before I got the mud off me and small rocks out of my ears. I had a few cuts and scratches on me and the crystal of my watch was broken.

MARIALICE ETEM

We were already in our basement when a friend of mine in Ruskin called and said she was coming over to our house in Hickman Mills because she didn't have a basement. I started sweeping up, tidying up the kid's mess. As I was doing that, a sifting of dust came down from the ceiling. That's what made me think there was a lot of wind upstairs. We did hear the roar but I didn't know what that was. I didn't realize how much damage was being done.

ELINOR STEINBRUECK

We got as far as the overpass near our house. The winds were getting strong and when my neighbor tried to back the car up a little, to get under the bridge more, the tornado stopped us. He couldn't get the car to budge. It just felt like it was going to take us right up. I told my girls to get down and not look out the back window, but it was hard to be heard. We didn't have time to panic though. When it was all over, the first thing we saw was the demolished car behind us.

MARJORIE LANGFORD
I heard it coming but I didn't want my son to be frightened, so I held him and bent over him. I was knocked out immediately. Marvin Jr. remained conscious but I slept through all of this.

WILLIS WATKINS
We could hear the house being torn apart, windows breaking, but we had no idea that the whole house was practically gone.

PETE KOTSIFAKIS
I knew we were going to hear a big roar because I had been reading about tornadoes. It sounded like a train with bad wheels coming above you, right on top of you. Then it felt like someone was holding a sand blasting machine in your face. My wife worried about the hot water heater across from where we were standing because it was dancing all over the place. It finally fell. All of a sudden it got quiet and I realized we were in the vacuum of the eye of the storm. We knew this wasn't the end of it so we braced ourselves and held the kids tighter so they wouldn't slip out. We couldn't control the dog though and I guess he'd had enough. He managed to get out of the basement. The high vacuum felt very strange. Because of the pressure it felt like your brains were oozing out of your ears.

ANNA LEE HEMBREE
My husband, daughter and I were in the car right beside the tornado. Where we should have turned left we turned right, so we were going to run right into it. So we stopped at a friend's house across from Burke school, but they weren't home and the door was locked. My husband tried to break the door open with his hand so we could get in. He was holding our daughter, so it was difficult. The wind came and just threw me all over that shrubbery in front of their house. By the time he got the door opened it was gone.

MARTA SCHMACHER
My mother, sister, aunt and I had started walking down the driveway, but we didn't have time to go anywhere so we laid down against a retaining wall. At one point I looked up and I could see a big red ball in the center of it, way up high. Mom said she saw the same thing. We had a basement, but the house fell into the basement so we turned out to be safer outside.

JUDY JONES HECKADON

Still holding me, Mom made it to the stairs just as it hit. Her slippers were blown off her feet and I was sucked out of her arms. I don't remember anything after that.

DONNA BRAMBLE WILLIAMS

All of a sudden we felt the car skidding. It was so dark we couldn't see anything but we could feel objects hitting the car. The adults told the four of us kids to put our heads down between our knees about the time the windows blew out. I looked up once out the back and saw things like tires and other debris being thrown up in the air. We must have been in the funnel at that time. I never saw the water tower, but I know we hit it because parts of the car were found up there and the car landed at its base. The inside of the funnel smelled terrible. I felt grit being driven into my skin and like my body was being ripped apart and all the skin pulled off. All I could think of was what the kids at school would say the next day when they found out I was dead. At that point I may have been the only one conscious. I was the only one who remembered the bottom of the car falling out.

LOREN GAYDUSEK

Our house was one of the few hit in Grandview. I didn't quite make it to the basement. I was at the top of the stairs inside the garage, holding my eighteen-month-old daughter across my body. My wife and two little ones were in the basement under a table, but I got caught at the door and pushed against it with my back so it wouldn't blow open. After it was over the door I was leaning against was broken in four places and the window panes were out of it. The pipe railing where I was leaning was moved over quite a bit. It wasn't the storm that moved that railing. It was me pushing so hard.

MIKE ANGOTTI

We had just got back to the store from our house when the tornado hit. My wife and three of the kids made it into the building, but I was out on the sidewalk with a daughter under each arm. There was an iron post there that I braced up against. My four-year-old was being blown away from me so I had to hold her by the hair. Even then she was blown straight out off the ground. The eight-

year-old was on the side next to the A&P, blowing into me. If I had
had to pull both of them toward me, I probably would have lost one
of them. I was turned so I could see my car lift off the pavement
and blow down to the other end of the shopping center. It had been
only ten feet away from me.

THELMA KIRKMAN
Richards-Gebaur was so close, and we were used to the sound of
jets going overhead all the time. We didn't think anything of it, but
this sound was like twenty or thirty jets roaring all at once. My
husband, Roy, grabbed me and we pulled the divan over to shield
us. We couldn't see anything, but we could hear the windows pop-
ping, just like glass popcorn.

BETTY HAMBEL
We ran to the bedroom and got down behind a dresser. I lay on
top of my son and my two girls were right behind me. My ex-husband, who was from out of town visiting the kids, shut the bedroom
door behind us and about that time the house exploded. The only
thing that went through my mind was how it would feel to fly out
the window. In a situation like that, you just go numb.

JOHNIE EAGER
My older brother Bill and I had been outside playing and saw it
coming before our parents knew about it. I waited to see it hit my
grade school, Burke, then ran downstairs into the basement. We
got there just in time. It sounded like you were in a wind tunnel, just
a howling kind of sound. Everyone says jet engines, freight trains, it
was just so loud, and the debris hitting the house combined with
the actual tornado sound was so frightening I forgot all about seeing my third grade class fly away.

AL CAUDLE
Since we were already in the basement of the Presbyterian church,
one of the other scoutmasters and I helped people get downstairs.
Just before it hit, Bud went upstairs to get more people and his
wife started up the stairs after him, screaming for him not to go.
When the tornado hit the church, I was trying to drag her back into
the basement and to tell you the truth, I didn't hear the roar of the
storm because Bud's wife was screaming right into my ear.

TREVA WOODLING

Harry got out on his side of the car and I got out on mine. All this, mind you, happened in just a matter of seconds. I stood with my back to the tornado, getting my three kids out of the car, and in my mind I was thinking I'd get them on the ground and lay on top of them. I didn't know what else to do. But I didn't even get a chance to tell them to lay down. I was screaming prayers all the time I was doing this, and yet I was aggravated with Harry in my mind because he wasn't helping me get the kids out of the car. I thought, Well, you chicken you. I thought he was on the ground, but he told me later the wind was blowing him all around and he had no control of where he was going.

I didn't see where Diane, who was almost five, and Dean, who was two, went, but I grabbed hold of our three-year-old Denise's arm. It just seemed like for a second or so time stood still and I looked at her face. Time was frozen. She was just petrified. I never will forget the look on her face. I had hold of her arm and the tornado sucked her up. I pulled her down and it sucked her up and I pulled her down again. It sucked her up a third time and I tried to pull, but God's angel just opened up my hand and I felt a voice saying, "Let go, I've got her." That's the feeling I had. It was like a spirit telling me.

Debris kept hitting me in the back. It felt like what I would imagine a machine gun would feel like, starting at my shoulders all the way down to my heels. I was knocked down to the ground and I couldn't move except to turn my head. I looked around and couldn't see my kids or my husband, but I saw our car being picked up with both doors open and blown away.

REV. LOREN GOINGS

There was a dinner meeting going on at our church (Ruskin Heights Baptist) that night so I was at the front door letting people from the neighborhood into the church basement. People were just pouring in. Just before it hit, there was hail that looked like it had been a round ball of ice and then flattened. There weren't very many of them but it was the strangest thing. I had never seen hail like that.

I watched it hit the shopping center a block or so to the west of the church. There were sparks of light. It looked like someone lighting matches. I was told later that when a power line goes down it tries to connect twice and if it doesn't connect then it cuts off. That's what I was seeing, like matches lighting up. I watched it go right by. It missed the church by a block, so I watched it go over to the northeast.

BLAINE STECK

I had started up the glass hallway from the gym to meet the nurse in her office. I heard a rumbling sound like a freight train, but of course we do have a train track just west of the school, so it didn't attract my attention that much. We have those sounds all the time. It got louder and louder and things began to hit the roof. Then I figured it was something serious so I headed back to the music room. By this time the glass hallway windows were breaking and crashing. I got inside the double doors of the music room and boy, I'm telling you, I can still hear stuff hitting that roof and the sound of all those windows breaking. I just ducked down right there in the corner. There was a wastebasket there, so I tried to get that over my head, which I did to some extent. I'll have to say, I did a little praying that the roof wouldn't cave in on me.

DIANE NEHRING LEVALLEY

I was the only one of us who made it to the basement. Just when I got to the church doors two men in Boy Scout uniforms grabbed me and threw me down the stairs. I was the last person to make it down there before the tornado hit. One of the men blew down the stairs with me and landed on top of me.

The other people in our car were still out on the church lawn. All of them were badly injured. My mother was carrying my little sister so she threw her down to the ground and laid on top of her. They were right outside the door.

AUDREY GERRED BECKLEY

As I was getting our four girls to go to the basement two doors down, I told them we were going to a party. I didn't want them to get upset. But when we got into the basement my youngest, who was only two, said she couldn't breathe and she panicked. All the kids were lined up against the wall with the adults in front. We had a pregnant woman and measles and whooping cough and a dog. All of us felt like the air was being sucked out of us. When my daughter said she was going to get out of there, I got her down on the floor in a hurry. I grabbed her leg and the tornado bounced us up and down just like it was a jack hammer. I lost fillings out of my teeth.

HELEN BOYLES

It made a horrible, horrible noise. For years I couldn't be around jet engines at the airport because it brought it all back, the horror you went through. There was also the sound of screaming and crying. Everybody was doing that. I know I screamed, "God save us." Then you heard the crash of everything hitting the house and flying by.

LOUIS MANNEN

I was a principal at a junior high in Independence, and I had a late meeting with a parent and teacher. As I was driving home on Noland Road, I pulled over to fix my windshield wipers. The car radio wasn't working, so I had no idea there was a tornado in the area. Just as I got back into the car I saw the tornado go across the road a little ahead of me. If I hadn't stopped I would have run right into it.

At our home in Ruskin, my wife heard the warnings on television. When she turned it off she could hear the roar. She got the kids in the hallway just in time. The tornado scooted them along the floor, and my wife and daughter were thrown in between the refrigerator and the bathtub when the walls blew away. A mattress came over the top of them and made kind of a cave of protection. My three-year-old son was thrown into the front yard and his pajamas were blown off.

PAT JARDES

We lived just a few blocks east of the shopping center, and the whole family was out in the yard. We heard what sounded like a very loud train and looked up in time to see a car hit the water tower. My husband yelled for us all to get in our car, but before we could the tornado went by. We were on the outer edge by a block or so and all it did was float my three-year-old son and me up a few houses then plop us in the neighbor's yard. None of us were hurt.

JEAN HAYES

Right before it hit, the air was so dead calm still it hurt. There were about twenty of us in the Millers' basement on the southwest corner of our block, and we could hear it coming. It was just like a freight train roaring at you. Someone said, "Here it comes," and then you heard nails being pulled right out of the walls upstairs and metal just absolutely tearing. It was so hard to breathe. No one screamed. We sat there horrified, and waited for it to pass.

The basement at the southwest corner of 110th Street and Sycamore sheltered most of my neighbors. Of the twenty or so people there, most were children, my playmates. The five below ranged in age from eleven to three, but all had similar memories.

STEVE GALLER

Our dog, Brownie, was the first into the basement, but I had to hold him because he was so nervous. The sound was awful, there could have been twenty jets taking off right in front of us from the way it sounded. It all happened so quickly, and mostly I was trying to control the dog, but I do remember the feeling of pressure in my head, like it was expanding, and of someone wanting to light a match to see, but everyone shouting, "No!" because of the escaping gas.

DANA GALLER CORDER

Everyone sat around the walls of the basement just holding one another. Some piece of debris, I think it was a piece of wood, flew through the room and landed just under my mother's arm and stuck into the wall. That and the sound of the walls upstairs being ripped apart left the biggest impression.

PAM POTTER SMITH

My dad was at work and my mother was so frightened. That scared me. I had never seen adults afraid before. I was three, so I didn't really understand much about what was going on, but my mother was scared, so my reaction was more because of hers.

CAROL HAYES

There was a horrible loud roar, louder than you can ever imagine, but the worst part was the feeling that all the air was being sucked right out of you. It was very hard to breathe. The air had an almost metallic taste to it and it was hard not to taste it.

PEGGY MCNAMARA

There was a lot of commotion. It was a large-size basement but it seemed crowded. Mom told us to put our heads between our knees and then she held all three of us together. All we could think of was the fact that Dad hadn't made it down the street in time. He was somewhere outside in all that awful noise. I couldn't breathe because dust kept going up my nose. My brother still says I was scream-ing, but I don't remember that. It just seemed to go on forever.

DAVID MILLIN

We hadn't been in the basement two or three minutes before it hit. My mother was sitting in a chair next to the wall on the garage side, holding my baby sister. I was on one side of the chair and my sisters on the other. Mom said she felt pretty silly being down there, that maybe we were overreacting. Then the lights flashed on and off a couple of times and it sounded like all the glass in the world was breaking right above us. As soon as it hit, Mom started saying the Lord's Prayer. We all joined in. I felt like I was being pulled back against the wall, and just assumed it was the tornado doing it. Af-terwards I found out it was Mom, holding on to my shirt.

DEAN AND NANCY EVANS

Dean: I headed east on Sycamore, going about sixty miles per hour, and ended up on Longview Road. There was a stream of traf-fic coming out of the Ruskin Shopping Center, so I just pulled out and made a second lane. We were going at right angles to the tor-nado. We got the impression it walked right up the edge of that horrible cloud we had seen in our front yard. I would not turn toward that thing under any circumstances. We got to a safe place and watched it go through Ruskin.

Nancy: I can still close my eyes and see the window frames of houses swing out the sides of the cylinder. That's what you could recognize. There was an awful lot of stuff flying around the base of it, but you could recognize window frames. It gave you chills to think about what you were seeing.

Dean: A guy pulled up right beside me. He yelled something at me and I yelled something back and we could not make ourselves heard.

Nancy: Up to that point, we were not particularly aware of noise, but then we realized it was a tremendous noise because they could not hear each other.

JEAN FROUNFELTER

All we had time for was to get over against the west wall, cover our heads, and pray. About that time we heard the sound of the house being pulled apart. You could hear the jumble of things crushed and moving, but the worst sound was the screeching of nails being pulled. We knew the house we were in was being destroyed. We had our dog with us and the noise was driving him crazy. My husband had to hold him, he was in such agony. He held the dog and I held the baby.

GLEN WILLIAMS
We felt just like we were being swooped up. The best way to describe the sensation is you felt like you were on the tail end of an airplane that was being shot off a carrier, just a whoosh, that's the sensation I remember. It took us out in the backyard and just constantly churned us up with debris hitting us the whole time.

MARY NORTHCRAFT
We went to the basement next door. As we were sitting down there, bracing ourselves for the worst, Clara, whose house we were in, came down the stairs with a pot of coffee for everyone. I guess the pot was on and she figured it shouldn't go to waste.

There were people stopping their cars out in front and running into the basement, total strangers, but we were glad to have them. When the tornado hit I had one son under me and Clara had our other under her. There was stuff flying around in the basement, including a replica of the submarine Clara's husband was on during World War II. Our neighbor from across the street was lying on the floor and when that submarine hit him he thought he was a goner. He never expected to be hit by a submarine during a tornado.

Some people were calm and some were hysterical. Clara's husband kept yelling, "Where's the hatchet?" and the lady who lived on the corner screamed, "Oh, Mama Mia!" over and over again. I'll never forget that.

JEAN MCCOY
We got the baby under the bed but we could only get our heads under. I remember thinking, Boy, this is a lot of hail. And then the windows started going and the ceiling fell down over us, making a sort of shield over the bed.

JAMES SHOOT
I was a truck driver and I had been making deliveries in Kansas that day, around Spring Hill and Ottawa. I missed all the heavy weather there and I didn't have a radio in my truck, so I had no idea

what was going on all around. It was my wife's birthday, so all I could think of was getting home, in Lee's Summit, to celebrate. I was going east on 63rd Street a little before eight o'clock and it was raining so hard I stopped the truck around Prospect. I had never seen rain so thick and dark. After a couple of minutes I started off again, and did fine until I got to Knobtown. There weren't many buildings in that area then, mostly woods, but I could see through the unusual lightning the outline of the tornado. It looked like a wide wall of water. It was the sound that gave it away. I saw power lines break and the tops of trees flying off and there was building material debris everywhere. I didn't know what direction that thing was going so I just kept heading for home. I was scared to death. I didn't know if I was running into it or away from it, and I didn't know if it had hit Lee's Summit. I didn't know it at the time, but I was just where it lifted back into the clouds for the first time in seventy-one miles. If I hadn't stopped for the rain, I would have run right into it.

I'm sure I broke every speed limit the rest of the way home. My family had watched the tornado as it moved across the horizon and they were still out in the yard. They heard my truck coming way before they could see me.

RICHARD McMILLIN

I was floating on Lake Tapawengo and I happened to look up at a dark cloud passing in my direction. At first this cloud appeared to have a streak in it, but as I watched I realized what I was seeing was a definite funnel. Then all of a sudden it turned in a horizontal plane and started to break up. Of course I found out later that night what a horrible path that tornado had caused. But I watched it die and disappear.

BILL MARTIN

I'll tell you one thing. If you're ever in one of those things you'll know it because of that whirling sound. It sounds like a freight train using all its power. But you'll never forget the sound, I can guarantee that.

THE LAST PEOPLE LEFT ON EARTH

IV

At first there was silence, breathless, terror-filled silence, as though the tornado had claimed all sound for itself. Then, as people let go of each other and opened their eyes, moans and cries punctured the striped air. Some made it out of houses and basements in time to see the twister roar off into the northeast, as it wrote its signature through another few miles of farmland and woods.

The tornado began for me when the screen blew off the window and fell across my bed, waking me up. The curtains, usually waving gently to me as I fell asleep, were being ripped out the window. My toys came to life, shuffling and jumping through the room. I remember seeing some cardboard grocery boxes flying out the window from their miniature grocery cart, and feeling the anger of any child whose right of possession is being challenged. I wasn't frightened but very confused and a little awestruck. Then I heard my frantic parents calling my name. I got out of bed and tried to open my door but the pressure in the house was still so great that I couldn't open it. I called out, "Here I am," and was rescued into the arms of my parents.

Although badly shook, we knew we were lucky. We were together and, except for a small cut on my forehead, uninjured. The neighbor we shared the hallway with soon found her husband and baby unharmed as well.

Our house, although severely damaged, still had some walls and part of the roof. There was glass, insulation and roofing tar everywhere, even in our clothes and hair. All our possessions were in piles throughout the rooms. But all of that was more interesting than scary to me. What did scare me was the gaping hole where the front door used to be, and all the twisted metal and spiked wood sticking out of the front of the house. Through that hole I saw an unrecognizable landscape. There were no houses, no trees, nothing but destruction. Through the frame of the hole I saw my father helping to carry a dead woman to a torn mattress. I sneaked back to my room and found my Sweet Sue doll. I didn't let go of her for the rest of the night, but cradled her close to me, my injured baby. She had a small chip missing from her forehead, just about where my cut was.

STANLEY JEPPESEN

I was covered with debris and couldn't move. I could see, but not move. I could hear Sheryl crying but I couldn't see her. At least I knew she was alive. I saw one of my brothers-in-law come out of the house and try to start his car. It was sitting on a pile of debris and it didn't have any tires, but he got it started and tried to drive off.

My injuries were made worse by the way I was carried out of there. I was carried in a blanket. I remember my brother-in-law Bob getting mad at the guys helping because he thought I should be carried out on a door. Well, they didn't know how badly I was hurt. There wasn't a spot on me that wasn't cut and both of my legs were raw. You get to a point of pain where you don't really feel anymore. It's a different feeling. I knew Bob was right about the door, but I couldn't tell anybody anything. Six guys carried me in a blanket to Highway 150, which was about a mile away.

Sheryl had a head injury, cuts in three or four places and a broken leg. She was taken first to Richards-Gebaur and then St. Joseph Hospital. In fact, everyone ended up at various hospitals that night with head injuries and broken bones. I was the only one they kept, so it was a couple of days before I knew everyone was all right.

I ended up in Olathe Hospital. I remember someone trying to take my shirt off to get an X-ray and the shirt sticking to my wounds, which hurt quite a bit. I looked down at my shirt and told the doctor to go ahead and cut it off of me because it was the same damn shirt I had on when I had the car wreck the year before. Why would I ever think of that?

Your pores open up and debris gets in. That's why the doctor wouldn't sew up my cuts. For a long time I had dirt work its way to the surface. It was a long time before I got a haircut because my head was so sore. The barber said he couldn't do much so I told him to just cut it close to my head and start over.

SHERYL JEPPESEN MCKINNEY

The next thing I remember was being in a car with my grandmother. She had broken ribs but didn't know it yet. I had no idea where my parents were, and I still didn't understand what had happened. I don't remember flying away from my dad, just being in this strange car with lots of dirt in my mouth and blood all over me. My leg felt like it had a huge band around it, and I was in a lot of pain. But the fact that I was with my grandma was comforting. We were very close.

The next thing I knew we were at Richards-Gebaur and someone was carrying me through double doors. They had taken me right out of my grandma's arms and I was screaming and throwing a fit. For some reason Grandma was taken to St. Joseph Hospital. Maybe they didn't have room there, or maybe they were only seeing the most injured, but all I knew was I was losing my Grandma now along with everything else.

CHARLIE COOK

During the visitation, one of my aunts came up to me and said, "I don't want to upset you, but we've just heard that Martin City and Hickman Mills have been hit by a tornado." We had left our kids with a baby-sitter so we rushed home, scared to death about them. We lived just east of Bannister Road and Hillcrest, and there was a policeman blocking that intersection. We told him we had to get to our house, to see if our daughters were all right, but he refused to let us through. I waited there, frantic with worry, until he started talking to someone else. Then I gunned the car right through the intersection.

Our house had very little damage, partly because I had a tile roof and not shingles. The girls and the baby-sitter were shook, but fine.

My next concern was the store. I tried to get through, but a National Guardsman stopped me. I told him I had to get through because I had property I needed to check on. His response was to cock his rifle. I said, "Maybe some other time."

Of course I was worried about Lowell too. I found out later that Charlie Knorr, the druggist across the street, had come over to Lowell and told him the tornado was coming, that they could outrun it in the car. Lowell, who was a big burly guy, stood there cutting a round of beef and smoking a cigar, said no, he'd ride it out. They found him under our new 6,000-pound dairy case. If he had just left with Charlie or had gone to the crawl space he would have been fine.

NORMAN CARON

I was patrolling the area around 85th and Holmes when I saw two station-wagons coming from the south, covered with mud and full of injured people. I gave them a police escort to Menorah Hospital. By that time I had received orders to pick up five other officers and return to the Ruskin area. We had a temporary command post set up at the Ruskin Center almost immediately, because I got there about an hour after the tornado hit and it was in operation then. Sheriff Owsley deputized the Kansas City police so they would have the legal right to perform police duties in the area.

My partner for the night was a policeman who lived in Ruskin. While we were rescuing people he was worried about his own family. We made it to his house but it was gone. So was his family. It was about two a.m. before he found them at a friend's house, uninjured.

Sometime during the night I was called to Highway 71 to help with traffic. The highway was only one lane each way, so it was our job to keep it clear for the ambulances. We'd ask people to pull off into the ditch, and if they objected we'd forcibly remove them from their cars. It wasn't good public relations, but very necessary in some cases.

By midnight the highway cleared, so we went back to the shopping center to do more rescue work. I didn't see any media there that night, and I wasn't aware of other police departments or the National Guard, but I know they were there. When something like this happens, boundaries don't count.

JIM AND AGGIE TURNBAUGH

Jim: I got the camera and a lot of film. Aggie and I jumped in our little yellow convertible and headed toward the tornado's path. We got as far as Truman Corners where it destroyed everything that was finished. At the intersection of Blue Ridge and 71 Highway there was debris everywhere, so we knew we weren't going to go any further. Already there were ambulances from Richards-Gebaur loading up injured. Aggie grabbed me and there was a little girl, the first fatality we saw, being put into an ambulance. That's when we realized what we were dealing with.

We walked into the Hickman Mills business area, taking pictures. We were pretty well known in the area because of the *Advocate*, so no one questioned us. They knew we weren't there to loot. We took pictures of Debacker Chevrolet, the Hickman Mills Bank, Lyon's Drug,

Crest Food Center and the new bowling alley that was to open soon. The man who owned the land the bowling alley was on also had a liquor store on the property, in a trailer. All of that was gone and the debris was burning. As we got up close to it, I realized those pop noises we were hearing were not liquor bottles but shotgun shells going off. We quickly got out of there.

Aggie: Jim's dad was city editor of the *Kansas City Times* then, and we knew he had been trying to get hold of us, so we got home about ten-thirty or eleven and I started making calls. Jim decided to go on to Martin City, because by that time we had heard it had been hit also.

Jim: I was able to drive into Martin City but I didn't get many pictures before the State Patrol ran me out. Even with my Missouri Press Association press card, which they decided not to honor, they wouldn't allow me to take pictures. An officer told me to leave or he'd shoot. I always take those words as being very sincere.

WALT BODINE

Randall Jesse, our news director, was out at the time that we were doing the earlier broadcasts, but he heard about the tornado and got in touch with us. He went straight out there to the scene and we sent engineers there to meet him. We started calling in people who were off duty, but at first it was just Bill Leeds, a copy boy, and myself in the news room. We didn't know who we'd need, but when a big story breaks you just need bodies. You don't know where you're going to put them yet, but you get them. Almost as they walk in the door, you know where to send them.

We went all evening long, just bulletin after bulletin. Some came from Randall and some came from what we could hear on the police-radio hook up we had in the studio. We just kept those bulletins flying.

One of our stagehands, Don Ray, rushed a mobile unit out to Ruskin Shopping Center, where Randall was broadcasting from, to deliver equipment. At that time the mobile units we used were new Packard hearse bodies because they were ideal for big equipment. As soon as Don emptied everything out he turned that car into an ambulance. He made several trips that night.

RUSS MILLIN

We all left our Optimist Club meeting and I drove as far as I could back to Ruskin. My house was about a block northeast of the high school, but I couldn't get anywhere near it because of the debris. It was such a shock to see the high school destroyed, even the gym. I jumped out of my car, leaving it running with the lights on, and ran down the street. Of course all the houses were leveled, and I was absolutely frantic by the time I got to my house. I lived next door to Harry Collier and he came up to me and said, "Your family's all right. They got out and were taken to one of your friend's house." That was such a relief.

There was no floor left in our house, just a beam going across the top of the basement with the floor lifted completely off. You could look right down into the basement at the scarred walls and all the debris thrown in there. It's a wonder they lived through it. Not a one was hurt. The house had just exploded. The explanation I received was that all our windows were closed, creating a vacuum. The destruction was overwhelming. All gone, nothing left, not even a pocket comb. Later we got stuff back from as far away as 140 miles, library cards and such.

I started helping others dig out. There was a little boy two or three doors up from us, a playmate of my son's, who was dead, and his mother was holding him. I stayed with her until the ambulance came, and then I left to look for my family. When I got back to my car, unbelievably, the lights were still on and the car was running.

DAVID MILLIN

As soon as it was over I looked up and instead of ceiling I saw clouds rolling by. There was debris all over us, mostly pieces of wallboard and other building materials, but there was part of a swing set that fell right in front of us. We heard our neighbors, the Colliers, calling to us from their basement next door, so I hollered back to them that we were all right. I got out of the basement by jumping from one pile of debris to another and then helped my mother and sisters out. Mom didn't want us moving around much because of all the live wires, so we stayed there with the Colliers for a while until someone from Reverend Collier's church picked us up to take us out of the area. We were all so dirty, with dirt just blown into our skin and hair. But the part I remember the most was the sight of those clouds just racing across the sky.

RUTH RAY

When it was all over, the Methodist church was still over our heads, so it proved to be a pretty good place to be. You're too shocked to have much of an impression. I had three kids I was trying to hold on to and it was so dark we didn't get the full impact then. But I could hear gas hissing and people yelling for help.

Our neighbor's car was destroyed, so we walked to Blue Ridge. There was a patrolman there and he just stopped someone coming across there and asked them to take us home, so they did.

My husband worked until nine-thirty. He didn't think there was any problem because they didn't mention Martin City on the radio accounts he heard. He couldn't believe it was as bad as we said it was because he drove in from the west and our house wasn't damaged at all. The next morning he drove down to Martin City, came back home, sat in his chair and shook.

DR. ALEXANDER SHIFRIN

I had just arrived for evening rounds at Menorah when the first victims arrived. The cafeteria, which was in the basement at that time, was immediately turned into a triage unit. Most of our doctors had some military training, but not necessarily combat training. Some had done this during the war and some hadn't. But we were all trained to handle any kind of emergency and everyone knew what to do. As an internist, it was my job to make a quick diagnosis, tag the patient and send them to surgery or orthopedics, where ever they needed to go.

I saw a lot of abdominal injuries, a lot of perforations of foreign matter. One of the patients I was assigned to had a large splinter in her skull. The patients I saw were all conscious and they let us know they were in pain, but no one was hysterical. Many were in shock, but emotional shock rather than physical.

WILLIS WATKINS

I didn't know if a tornado had an eye like a hurricane so we stayed put, thinking maybe there was a trailing edge coming. Then I smelled gas and I thought, "Boy, we better get out of here!" The gas meter was right outside the corner where we were, and the entrance to the crawl space was a step going out of the house to the garage. I got over there and tried to lift the door but I couldn't because of the debris on top. That was really the scary part. Before that I didn't have time to feel scared. I suppose the adrenaline started pumping, and I got a shoulder against it and got it pried open enough to get an arm out and started pushing stuff aside. The refrigerator had fallen right beside the door.

We were relieved to get out of the crawl space, but the scene upstairs was unreal. Some of the horns from cars at Debacker Chevrolet were set off when the cars were tossed around, and that sound was weird. We came up out of there and the only sound we heard was those horns.

Most of the gas meters were broken off and gas was hissing everywhere, but I went around and turned off valves where there were still values to turn off. Some that were broken off below the valve, I tried to stuff with rags and sticks because I was worried about fires breaking out.

People in the area who didn't live here were stopping and picking people up. Someone told us to walk up to the corner and we'd get picked up, which is what we did.

It was amazing that you could walk through and not step on any nails, because when you came out the next day and looked at the stuff, there were nails sticking up everywhere.

CLYDE RENKEN

All the basement windows were jammed full of trash and dirt. We got over to the basement door to go up, but the vacuum of the tornado had pulled the basement door casing over and jammed it down inside the basement stairway. We didn't have a way out.

Finally I went and got a hammer and screwdriver and took pins out of the basement door to take it off. Then I had to stand there and throw all of the debris up out of the basement stairway before we could even get out.

When we got upstairs everything was gone. The house down to the floor was just as slick as it could be. All we had was what was on our backs. We were stunned. We didn't know what else to do, so we went across the street to see what was happening. Cars couldn't go up and down the street on account of the debris. We couldn't have gotten out anyway because we found our car up the street, thrown in back of the houses into some woods.

Then some kid came running down the street and said that there was another one coming in the same path. We thought Well, there's nothing to do here, so we walked up to the corner to see if we could hitchhike a ride into town.

My brother-in-law was sitting out on his porch in town listening to the radio and heard there was a tornado in our area. He didn't even wait for my sister. He jumped into the car and came on out here. He got over to our street before the highway patrol had it blocked off, so he drove right up to our corner, saw us, and took us to their house.

JOE NESBIT

We couldn't get back to our house so we decided the best thing to do was for my wife and kids to go her parent's farm. After my family left, I walked up to Burke school, where I was principal, and looked around. I guess I was just sort of dazed and overwhelmed by the damage it had done to the school. After awhile, I went back home and tried to get some rest, but I had to clean up first. There were holes where two-by-fours had gone through the roof. Fortunately it didn't rain that night. I remember shaking glass off the bed onto the floor and sweeping up a little. I went to bed but I couldn't go to sleep, so after awhile I got up, dressed and went back up to the school. I could hear water running, so I shut the water to the building off and turned the gas off. I don't know how long I stayed around there, but I know I went back to the house around three a.m.

Very few people, as I recall, were out when I went home the second time. There was an eerie stillness to the whole scene. The National Guard had moved in, and I remember a guardsman on the corner of 113th and Bennington stopped me. But I convinced him that I was not a sightseer and that I lived down there and I was on my way home. I was just dumbfounded and dazed by the scope of destruction, and that was just in Hickman Mills.

I saw people that night and, they tell me now, I talked to them but I don't remember at all. I was in shock.

SIDNEY BATES

All the windows collapsed on the southeast side of Burke school and the ceiling dropped into the gym, but our scout troop was on the other side of the school and no one was hurt. There was a janitor who was injured and we helped him as best we could.

The scene outside was unbelievable. Everything looked sandblasted and pockmarked. There was so much debris in that storm that everything was covered with gray dirt. It was like everything had lost its color, like a moonscape.

We knew another Boy Scout troop was having a meeting at the Presbyterian church, and it looked like the tornado had gone that way, so we walked up there. That was our church and I had good friends in that troop, so we were sick to see it flattened. Fortunately, we found out quickly that everyone who made it to the church basement was O.K. But there were a lot of injured lying on the lawn and our scout leaders offered help. There was so much that needed to be done, we didn't know where to start. I remember being disturbed, not knowing what I should do.

The eerie calm was spooky. No one was hysterical. There was talk about gas mains blowing up, but a lot of people just seemed to have a dazed response, like the worst had already happened to them, they couldn't be worried about gas leaks.

LOREN GAYDUSEK

We just had to get out of our neighborhood so I went down Third Street, which was Gardner at the time. Somebody said, "I can't find my husband." I started looking for him with some other people and found him laying under the side of a garage. He was dead when we found him.

MARJORIE LANGFORD

The neighbors across the street knew that my son and I were home, so they came quickly after it was over. Marvin Jr. was able to move a stick to let people know where we were. The tornado had blown a refrigerator in on me. However, there must have been other stuff too, because if a refrigerator had hit me straight on, I'd have been gone. They got a door to carry me out on because I was unconscious and they didn't know the extent of my injuries. A station-wagon came by and the neighbors got me in there and took me to the hospital.

Marvin Jr. remained conscious all this time, so the neighbors took him to a doctor in Grandview and turned out he had a broken arm and bad bruises.

My husband did not know there had been a tornado because he didn't have the car radio on. But as he was coming back from teaching a night class in the city, he couldn't believe how people were driving. He knew there was something going on, and of course when he got to a certain point they stopped him and wouldn't let him in. He identified himself and showed where he lived and they let him come in. By that time we were gone, and the remaining neighbors said they were taking most people to Menorah Hospital. He liked to never get out of the area for, as he called them, the wicked sightseers. Now, they might not have all been sightseers. I'm sure some of them were trying to get home or to get to relatives.

I was at Menorah. The man driving the station-wagon just wanted to get me to the hospital as soon as he could, and that was Menorah. When my husband finally found me, I was laying on a dining room table because they were so crowded. They had sewn a big gash on my forehead up with black thread. My husband later told me there was crying and moaning there at the hospital, but it was not the people who were injured. It was the relatives.

I was in and out of it for a week. My injuries were mostly head and neck, with a concussion and skull fracture and all kinds of neck injuries. At some point they moved me to St. Luke's, but I stayed in the hospital for a month.

I do remember being conscious at one point. A priest was going around and he came up to me and asked if I was Catholic and I said no. A little later he came by again and asked. When I said no this time he said he was going to pray for me anyway.

Some of the first casualties were taken to the dispensary at Richards-Gebaur Air Force Base. Medical corpsmen and other physicians worked continuously with the chief base physician, Dr. Alfred Michael, throughout the night. Dr. Michael's wife checked patients in and acted as a triage assistant before the night was over. She reported eight dead. They did what they could with limited space and supplies and sent some patients to other hospitals.

MARIALICE ETEM

I didn't realize until we got up the basement steps how awful it was. I thought a tree would just be knocked down or something like that. The whole house was gone, completely gone. We found splinters of the crib our eighteen-month old son had been asleep in just moments before the tornado hit in the front yard.

As soon as my husband knew we were all right, he took off. I thought, "How can he leave me at a time like this?" He said he knew we were O.K. but that there were people out there hurting. He was the insurance agent in Hickman Mills and, after us, his first thoughts were about his clients. Right away he found the Schumachers, who were all injured and in their driveway.

So I gathered the kids together. Now, they had their night clothes on because we went to bed early, and they were barefooted. I didn't find shoes for the kids until the next day. I didn't pick up anything, just the kids. There was one house left on the corner. I decided we'd walk down there, I didn't know what to do. Here I had these five little kids, from seven years old to eighteen months, and we walked across the yards, barefoot, where there were live wires, glass and all kinds of debris. And do you know, not one of them got so much as a scratch.

All the neighbors were assembled at this house on the corner and we went down to their basement. By that time people were screaming and crying, and the children were all upset, and there were rumors of another tornado coming. That was really horrible.

PETE AND DOROTHY KOTSIFAKIS

Pete: I opened my eyes and on top of me I saw the floor overhang and I was confused because I thought it was the overhang of the front end. Then I thought, no, those are floor joists, so I looked up and there, unbelievably, were stars. Then we heard a big bang and saw a flash as the filling station up by Ruskin exploded.

We wanted to get out, but we were afraid to move. There was the sound of sizzling wires and of gas escaping as we crawled out. Originally, we had planned on getting under a workbench in the southwest corner of the basement, but our son, who was still in diapers, was scared to go under it, so we went in the closet under the back step instead. It's a good thing we did. The house collapsed into the basement, including the bathtub, and the only place not full of debris was in the closet.

When we crawled out where the window used to be, it looked like a bomb had hit this area. When we bought this lot there were twenty-five trees. I think there were three standing and we lost them too. There wasn't any bark on them, and there were cars wrapped around them.

When Wilson Hembree, my next door neighbor, came back, I hollered over to him that I thought too much gas was escaping. He didn't care about that. He was looking at his shrubbery and saying, "Look at my beautiful shrubbery. You saw me out here watering it and now it's all gone." That just shows you that at first you can't believe that it was happening. It took a little time to even believe it.

When you looked around and saw all that mess, you figured might as well move. If they gave you ten years to clean your lot out you couldn't do it. That's how we felt that night.

Dorothy: There was a report going around that there was another tornado coming. Some people from across the street came to their doorway— their house wasn't as badly damaged— and said to come on over there, that we could go down in their basement. So that's where we went. I had no more diapers for our son, but these people had towels hanging on a clothesline there in the basement, so that's what I used.

Pete: When another tornado didn't come we got our wits about us and went back out to look for more people. A car came by, and a guy asked if he could help anybody, and I said, "Yeah, can you take my wife and three kids to her mother's house?" He says, "Of course." As they drove off I thought, "I just gave my whole family to a stranger," but they got there O.K.

ANNA LEE HEMBREE

We couldn't get back to our house. Judy and I stayed where we were when it hit and Wilson walked back. Eventually Wilson's brother and wife got through to us and Judy and I went back with my sister-in-law while Wilson and his brother spent the rest of the evening looking for anything of ours they could find. Our house had enough jagged walls left that we could get into closets and maybe find some things, but they were just ruined.

He told me later that it was not what he did see but what he didn't see that was so upsetting. Nothing was there anymore. Of course the whole scene there in Hickman Mills was scary that night. Car horns were stuck and sirens could be heard everywhere but there was a horrible stillness too.

Meanwhile, Judy got deathly sick. She went into shock and was throwing up so much we took her to a doctor in Raytown. It was a couple of days before I even saw what was left of our house.

MARTA SCHUMACHER

Our neighbor, Mr. Etem, helped dig us out from under the debris and get us a ride to the hospital. All of us, Mom, my sister, my aunt and I ended up in the hospital.

My uncle and brother had gone to Warrensburg on a service call and didn't know anything about it until they got back. When they saw the area, my brother Fred jumped out of the car before Uncle Fred could even get the truck stopped. Somebody told my brother we had all been taken to the hospital. They finally found us at Research and checked on us before heading home. Well, the police wouldn't let them back in. They arrested both of them, thinking they were looters. One police officer hit Fred over the head with a flashlight and when he came to, he had handcuffs on.

JUDY JONES HECKADON
When Mom, Grandma and my sister came out of the basement our house was gone and they couldn't find me anywhere. Then Mom heard me crying. She found me out in the front yard underneath a bathtub. We don't know if I blew into it and then it overturned or if it fell over me. Miraculously, it didn't fall on me. None of my arms or legs were injured. I had grit and pebbles blown into my skin and that had to be removed, but the tub protected me from everything else.

DONNA BRAMBLE WILLIAMS
I hit the ground somewhere in back of Burke school. I couldn't see anybody, although I wasn't buried in debris. I guess I was laying on top of a lot of stuff. I called for my mother and heard Dick's voice calling back, "Who's yelling?" So I knew he was O.K. and Jay was there too. I couldn't get up because my back was broken. My arm was twisted backwards, so I knew it was broken too.

When rescuers came we told them to look for the others, and finally the car was found at the base of the water tower. Corky was still inside. They didn't tell me for a week that she was dead. Mom was on the ground and still alive, but she had nothing but blood the whole length of her body. She looked like someone had taken a knife and ran it down her body. She was unconscious and had head injuries too. It's almost too much to think about, even now.

Jay didn't wake up until he was in the hospital. He had a collapsed lung, punctured bladder and a horrible leg injury. It literally looked like his leg was hanging on by a thread.

It was the next day before they found Cathy, the older Davis girl, dead underneath the water tower.

GENE AND MARJORIE MONTEE
Marjorie: When the tornado passed there was no drugstore. The whole front of the store had caved in on our new car. If they hadn't

gotten the phone call and looked out the back door of the pharmacy, the boys and I would have been sitting in the car. A man was killed two cars down from us. When we came out he was slumped over his steering wheel.

Gene: We got up out from underneath all this stuff and of course we were just saturated with insulation because that stuff just eats into your body. Then we were concerned about electrical wiring. There were wires laying everywhere, and we didn't know if they were live or not. You had to be very, very careful where you stepped for fear of being electrocuted after going through all that.

We came out of there with very minor scratches. Our son, Nick, had a scratch on his hand that was bleeding, but when we think about how close we came to being killed we really feel the good Lord had his hand on our shoulders that night. If we hadn't stopped for the medicine, we would have been right around the shopping center or the water tower at the time the tornado hit. You know, we never did get that medicine.

So there we were, our car destroyed, our home too far away to walk to and no way of getting across the debris to it anyway, two sick boys. We were trying to figure out what to do next when a car pulled in and total strangers asked us if they could give us a ride somewhere. We figured out real quick that we couldn't get to our house, so I said I wanted to go to Union Station. We got on the midnight train and went to Pittsburgh, because that's where we're from.

I'm surprised I had enough money on me, because in those days you didn't carry credit cards, but I bought four tickets. Since we're from Pittsburgh, Kansas, we knew a lot of the railroaders. Turns out, on that particular train the engineer and conductor were old friends of ours. So they wanted to know all about it and we told them. As they went through Ruskin on the Kansas City Southern tracks, which go right behind the shopping center, they just crept through there. Debris had been cleared from the tracks already, and we were able to see it all from an elevated point. It looked like a war zone. There were ambulances and fire trucks and police and what looked like thousands of cars trying to get down Blue Ridge. Oh, I mean, it looked like a human anthill, with cars swarming everywhere. In fact, car headlights provided most of the light in the area. But the destruction was just immense from where we were. Houses blown apart, trees stripped, mangled cars really did remind me of landscapes I'd seen during World War II.

The man we sold our house to didn't know where we were or even if we'd been killed. We had no way of contacting him. We didn't really know him, because we'd just closed the deal that morning. He couldn't get over there to see his property and he didn't know where to find us. Until we finally got hold of him the next day, that poor man was going out of his mind.

MIKE ANGOTTI

I found my wife and other kids just a few feet inside the store. We were very lucky that nothing heavy had fallen on them, or that they weren't badly cut. The eight-year-old daughter, who had been next to A&P, had some pretty deep lacerations on her back, and we had to take her to the doctor in Grandview, but she was the only one who needed medical attention. The windows had all blown out and the roof was lifted off then set back down. I lost some inventory, but not everything.

There were rescuers there digging people out almost immediately. The A&P was particularly hit. Fortunately, most of the stores were closed at that time of night, but I know Ben Franklin and Crown Drug were open. We had so much to take care of, and without light it was hard to know what to do first. We took care of our daughter first, but after we got back from the doctor's I went back to the store and was there well past midnight. Our house wasn't damaged, so my wife stayed with the kids there.

Everything happened so fast that during the tornado I didn't have time to be scared. Afterwards, when I saw that we were all alive and realized how much destruction there was around us, and that people had died just a few yards away from us, that's when I got frightened. That's the trouble with thinking.

JOHNIE AND BILL EAGER

Johnie: The tornado lifted up a corner of our foundation, threw a bunch of debris in there, cut us up a little, then pushed the foundation back down. Afterwards we could hear it rumbling off in the distance but we were so stunned we just sat there for a while. When we came out it was dark, and we could still see the funnel off to the northeast when there was lightning. We got to see it coming and going.

It was such an eerie scene. As we looked across Blue Ridge at the old high school it looked like a shell. The front wall was partly stand-ing, but the back part was completely gone. And the new high school looked like a bomb had gone off. The silhouette of the gym girders in the dark made us feel like we were in a war.

Bill: When we came up out of the basement it looked like a plane had flown over and dumped trash everywhere, or a big plow had come through and pushed everything down. It smelled like death. Our dad had been in Europe during World War II and he said it had the same feel and smell.

We stood out front for a while, trying to figure out what to do next. About a half hour had gone by and I noticed a girl walking down Blue Ridge. She was coated with blood and just walked on like a zombie, not asking for help. I recognized her because I had seen her many times working behind the soda fountain at Crown Drug.

Johnie: Our car was in the driveway, an old Nash. Of course, all the windows were broken out of it, and there was a two-by-four running through the backseat where it kind of pushed one of the doors about a third of the way across the backseat. Once we knew we were O.K. and our house was livable, our first response was to check on friends outside the neighborhood. The phones were out, so we had to drive. I remember getting into the car that night and we were driving around with no windshield. When we came back in at first we were afraid the National Guard wouldn't let us in. But they looked at our battered car and said, "I guess you guys are O.K., go on, I don't think you're faking it."

In less than ninety minutes, seventy police reservists joined those Kansas City policemen already on duty. Although the disaster area was not within the city limits, Mayor H. Roe Bartle and Major Donald Bishop mobilized the city's police force to help, because help was desperately needed. Ambulances were located, including four in stor-age at an ambulance dealer's garage, and sent as quickly as pos-sible to the scene. When ambulance drivers could not be found, police officers were given authorization to drive.

Police dispatchers, receiving scores of desperate messages from the field, had to untangle the lines of communication and see to it that all were helped. Too often they had the sad task of reporting that there were no more ambulances available, that policemen would have to use station-wagons and private cars to transport the in-jured and homeless.

Policemen O. Dennison's plea for help was heard more than once by dispatcher Leo LaGrasso. Although Dennison's Hickman Mills home lay exposed and heavily damaged, the rescue of his neighbors came first. As more injured were discovered, his concern for friends came across in the frantic edge of his voice.

Even seasoned officers couldn't hold down the emotion in their voices. One, who was stationed just east of the high school, succinctly described the scene and his horror of it: "I need light and help to dig people out. The houses are completely down and no one is moving."

Dispatchers had lots of bad news that night. Shortly after police arrived, they started reporting that there were rumors of more funnels on the way. Although unsubstantiated, the rumors persisted and the dispatchers had to keep close to the weather teletypes as well as stay in contact with their patrolmen. They also had the duty of passing on what others did not want to hear. Looking for a gathering spot for survivors and injured, some officers suggested the high school. Others had to report, through the dispatchers, that the high school was flattened, that it was gone.

CHARLES GRAY

We got as far as 87th and Blue Ridge before a police blockade stopped us. I left my wife in the car to man the radio and started out on foot. Lucky for me, Jackson County Sheriff Arvid Owsley drove by about then in an unmarked station-wagon and offered me a ride into Ruskin. Since the devastated area was not part of Kansas City at that time, Sheriff Owsley was really the man in charge of all police operations. Even he had a hard time getting to the scene. One very nervous Kansas City policeman stopped us and tried to keep us from going any further by drawing his gun.

I had some friends at 106th and Eastern that I wanted to check on, and I needed to accumulate reports to take back to the car, so I was on my own once we got to the scene. After I found out my friend's house was undamaged, I walked along Blue Ridge. The only light was from searchlights and there was danger of stepping on live wires and debris. I could barely see the skeleton of the high school gymnasium and nothing beyond that. I ended up at the shopping center where I heard Mayor Bartle call out the National Guard.

It was hard to take it all in. Everywhere there was mass confusion. As I walked along Blue Ridge, I saw convoys of cars leaving the area, station-wagons with injured piled in anywhere they could fit. In many cases, traffic going the other way kept them from getting through, and I couldn't help thinking there might be people who wouldn't make it because of time lost.

When I got back to the car, I had a hard time getting my reports through by car phone. At that time there were only two noncommercial phone channels. One for the Red Cross and one for the Salvation Army.

BLAINE STECK

I had debris all over me. Especially tar from the school roof that just went everywhere. I stepped out into the hallway from the band room. To get out of there I really had to push that door hard because of the debris piled up against it. I opened that door and I'd say the hallway was filed up with everything. Not just building materials, but everything—tires, pieces of furniture.

My first thought was of Mrs. Guyall. So I tried to go up to the entrance of the school to see if she was O.K. I waded through material, about seventy-five to one hundred feet. Of course when I got up there I couldn't see anything. The roof was gone, and most of the walls, and I knew there wasn't any use trying to find anyone because it was dark and the halls were piled high. They found her later that night buried by the entrance. The janitor was a few yards away from her, also dead.

Before Mrs. Guyall was found I went across the street because I heard someone crying for help. There was a woman who was all right, but several of her family were missing. When I realized I couldn't help her because my car was destroyed and there were no phones, I decided I better walk home to check on my wife.

When I got home she looked at me— I looked a mess— and asked, "What happened to you?" And I said, "Well, we had a tornado." She wasn't aware that a tornado had gone through. The lights had gone off, but she was studying and just lit a candle and was reading in the kitchen by candlelight. She had no idea what had happened. We were just lucky it missed our house by a couple of blocks.

AUDREY GERRED BECKLEY

The stairway up out of the basement was clogged with debris, so three of the men, including my husband, crawled out the basement window. They could hear a woman who lived behind us crying for help, so they pulled her out of her destroyed house and handed her down to us through that window. This lady's husband was a policeman, and he was at work, so she was there at home with her two kids. The kids weren't hurt, but her legs were pretty badly cut. We doctored her the best we could there, and then one of the men, whose car still ran, took her and her kids to Richards-Gebaur's hospital.

When my husband first got out of the basement he went up to our house and found our dog, dead, where the garage had been. He didn't want the girls to see, so he found a hole across the street and buried him before we came out.

I thought I smelled gas, so we all crawled out the window. When we got out, one of my daughters said, "Are we the last people left on earth?" Across the street, where some of the people in the basement lived, was flattened. We just couldn't believe the destruction. Our first thought was to go up to the A&P store and call our families, but when we got in front of the high school, Blaine Steck was coming out and he told us he'd heard Ruskin Center was gone too. Blaine thought my husband was still in the school building and, of course, Glen thought that Blaine was caught in there. They were so glad to see each other that they hugged.

But without the shopping center we had to find another place to call from, so we walked up to the fire station, all twenty-five of us. When we got there we realized we couldn't take the kids in because there were covered up bodies lying on the lawn. My husband and I had just met the couple who lived next to the fire station, Dr. Alshe and his wife, so we went into their house. Dr. Alshe was at the station seeing people, but his wife graciously let us come in, all of us. We just sat in her front room and tried to figure out what to do next. She told me later that she liked to never get all the glass and stuff out of her carpet.

My husband was the only one with change in his pockets, because he hadn't been home long enough to empty his change out onto his dresser, so he walked on further looking for a phone that worked. He had a list of people to call and he had to walk quite a ways up Blue Ridge.

Eventually, his father picked us up, and the girls and I went into town. Glen and another man then walked the school district, checking on school damage for most of the night.

I just couldn't get that first image out of my mind. Coming up out of that basement, seeing all those flattened houses across the street, you did feel like you were the only people left in the world. It's such a lonely feeling.

DIANE NEHRING LEVALLEY

It seemed like we were trapped in that church basement for a long time, but it was probably only minutes before someone dug us out. Right away, my sister was brought down. She was very badly cut and had blood all over her. It was terrifying to see her that way. Everyone was pretty frantic and some man asked me to clean her up because she was my sister. I just ran away. Fortunately, a lady came to my rescue, I think it was our neighbor from behind, and took care of me. I just remember there were a lot of people in that basement and they all were very anxious to get out.

I stayed close by this neighbor lady, but after a while my sister was taken to the hospital and everyone was leaving. No one could tell me where my mother was, and I didn't know what was going to happen to me. There was a policeman there who was told I was by myself. He wanted me to go with him to the police station, but I threw such a fit that the neighbor lady said she'd take me with them.

We went back to their house, but it was too badly damaged to stay there. We ended up across the street from our backyard neighbors, because their house wasn't in too bad a shape. I needed to be cleaned up. I had cuts from flying glass and was bloody and dirty. So I spent the night there with people I didn't know.

I remember laying there that night and wondering where my mother was, and why my dad hadn't come for me, and what was going to happen to my sister. I don't think I got much sleep.

AL CAUDLE

When we came up out of the church basement we were shocked to see that the church was gone. All the lumber was laying there in the parking lot. It looked like the tornado had stacked our church up in the parking lot like cordwood.

My car was parked between the church and the high school and it was totally destroyed, so there was nothing for me to do but stick around and help. There was a family who got caught right by my car. They had a son at the scout meeting, and they were trying to get to the church basement. The mother was laying on the ground moaning, and the dad was walking in circles. The kids were nowhere to be found. Fortunately, they turned up later at the fire station. Anyway, someone came by and wanted to pick the mother up and take her to the hospital. But the scouts knew that she shouldn't be moved until she could have something solid under her. So they brought a tabletop up out of the church basement and carefully lifted her onto that table before putting her into the station-wagon. It turned out she had broken ribs and one had punctured her lung. The doctor said that she would have died if the Boy Scouts hadn't treated her so gently.

Other boys got busy plugging up the gas lines with mud or sticks or potatoes, anything they could find. But the most famous Boy Scout of the city was right in there with the rest of us. Before the night was over, I saw Mayor H. Roe Bartle directing traffic at Blue Ridge and 110th Street.

As soon as he received word of the disaster, Kansas City Mayor H. Roe Bartle left the annual trustees meeting of the Midwest Research Institute, held at the Hotel Muehlebach downtown. His special car was equipped with a three-way radio, a siren and emergency light. He sped to the scene and was there by eight-thirty. Although none of the devastation was within the Kansas City limits, Bartle immediately called for eighty percent of on-duty officers to report to the area. He also asked all off-duty police, firefighters, and municipal employees from the public works and water and parks departments to report as soon as possible. In a letter to Senator Stuart Symington for the Congressional Record, *Bartle spoke of "...hysteria in its worst form. No bombed area in any section of the world could have been more chaotic....Men and women were digging with their hands in the debris in hundreds of homes looking for those who were injured or dead."*

As rumors of looting spread, Bartle spoke through a loudspeaker: "This area is under martial law. There is live ammunition in these guns. If the men order you to halt, for God's sake do so."

REV. HARRY DALE COLLIER

Considering the destruction above us, we had little trouble getting out of the church basement. But the scene that greeted us was almost too much to comprehend. There was a church member who was injured on the lawn and I stayed with her and her husband until they were taken to the hospital. Then I headed for my house and family, afraid of what I might find. It took me almost an hour to walk the two blocks home. Along the way I found a Bible laying on the ground. I picked it up and carried it the rest of the night. When I finally reached home, my family was sitting on the garage floor. Floor was about all that was left.

After getting them taken care of, I went to all the Kansas City hospitals looking for injured church members. At Menorah I was asked to come into the morgue and identify victims. It was there I saw our neighbor boy, my son's playmate, who had been killed by their freezer. I also found a new Ruskin resident who had been killed on the church grounds. She had urged her two daughters to run ahead of her to the church basement and I had seen them there, so I knew they were safe. But up until that moment I didn't know what had happened to her. It was a night that has haunted me.

TREVA WOODLING
I was knocked out for I don't know how long, but when I came to I was yelling for Harry. He heard me and crawled over to where I was. I couldn't move. Everyone who came up out of the Presbyterian church basement thought I had a broken back.

Diane was found down close to the basement door, standing up, with her arms around another little girl. My next door neighbor saw her and carried her down to where Harry and I were. He laid her down beside me and she was crying with leg pain. I told her to lie down, she'd feel better, but she said, "I can't Mommy, it hurts too bad." I managed to move a hand to pat her on the leg and console her, and I kept telling her we were going to get help, that it would be O.K. Somebody found the back of a kitchen chair and shoved it into the ground so she could lean against it. That helped some.

After people kind of shook off the shock, there was a lot of activity, we could hear but not move to see. We heard people yelling, "Go shut off the gas over there, be careful of the power lines, get blankets, we need lots of blankets." People were scurrying everywhere.

A priest came up and asked if we were Catholic and we said no. He asked if he could pray for us anyway and Harry said, "Sure, it wouldn't hurt."

Harry sat next to me, not moving. People kept throwing blankets over him and he'd say, "Get that blanket off of me!" He had three sticks driven into his back and others stuck into his arm. His right ear was split almost in two. Because he wasn't moving, people thought he was in shock, so they'd cover him with a blanket but that just made him hurt more.

A man with a station-wagon came up to us and said he had plenty of room to take Harry and Diane to the hospital. Because of my back, no one wanted to move me. Harry said no, he wasn't leaving his wife. The man kept at us and wanted at least to take Diane. So finally Harry said O.K. The man asked what hospital did we want her taken to and Harry said, "The best one in Kansas City." He never did tell the driver which one he meant.

LOUIS MANNEN

As I drove on down Noland Road toward home, I saw a family walking down the road whose house was destroyed. I offered to give them a ride, never imagining my own family needed help. I dropped them off where they could get help and headed west on Bannister Road. By the time I got to Blue Ridge the traffic was so congested I couldn't go south, so I continued on Bannister to Highway 71. I ran into the same problem there, so I parked the car and walked to my house.

By the time I got there, my family was gone. A neighbor had taken them to a doctor in Grandview, but no one could tell me that then. The house was destroyed and the neighborhood deserted and I had no idea where my family was. I walked to the fire station on Blue Ridge but there was no sign of them there. Finally I went back to my car and drove to my mother-in-law's. I found everyone there, bandaged and shaken, but all right. Those were horrible hours.

HELEN BOYLES

There were about fifty people in the basement across the street. We couldn't get out the stairs because there was a car pushed against the door in the garage. So the men crawled out the window wells and the women and children stayed in the basement. The men went around the neighborhood looking for injured and then passed them down to us through the window. We had plenty to do taking care of the kids and the injured. I remember we tore off strips from our slips to use as bandages. We had no water or medical supplies.

It was a couple of hours before they got the car away from the doorway enough for us to get out of the basement. We couldn't see much because it was so dark, but my husband said, "Don't look." The house was leveled. We lost everything. Even the pieces of linen or clothing we found we had to throw away because they were so full of tar. I was able to salvage one picture album and some silver. Libby had one doll left. A neighbor had found it and put it on their car to give to Libby, but Libby saw it first and took it.

Our car, the one my husband was selling to our neighbor when the tornado came, was ruined in the driveway. My husband couldn't resist saying to the neighbor, "I'll sell it to you cheap."

We didn't know what to do. We ended up making a list of phone numbers people there wanted called, and we walked up to the fire station at Blue Ridge and Craig Road. They were tending the injured and sending them to hospitals, but their phones didn't work either so my husband kept walking north on Blue Ridge until he found a phone. That way he was able to call everyone's relatives.

LEON FELSON

A little after eight o'clock, I received a call from the switchboard people— whom I had routinely notified of my whereabouts— informing me there were some cars blocking the driveway to the emergency entrance. Since there was no personnel I could dispatch to take care of duty, I decided to go down and straighten it out myself. So I leisurely tossed my raincoat on and went down to the emergency area.

When I entered the lobby of the emergency room there suddenly appeared fifteen children laying on the floor. One in the corner was dead. In the emergency room itself, a child was on the floor with a pediatrician over the child giving artificial resuscitation. The only personnel in the area at that time was one nurse and one pediatrician.

For about one minute I was completely stunned, overwhelmed by the gravity of the situation, overwhelmed by children with head wounds looking up at me, not making a sound, by the grayness of the skin of the patients, completely at a loss to explain how such a thing could suddenly happen with no advance notification.

JEAN HAYES

We could smell gas in the basement. My husband, Vernie, went over to the window and ripped out the casement. George Miller, whose basement we were in, said, "What are you trying to do, tear up my house?" Vernie turned around and told him, "Hell man, you don't have a house."

We got everybody out of the basement through the window. It was just absolutely devastating to look around. You were afraid to walk because of the wires, splinters, glass, boards, just every imaginable kind of debris. We went out the Sycamore side and walked around the corner in the street. You could avoid things better that way.

When we got to our house the garage was the only thing intact. But I wouldn't let Vernie open it because the garage door handle was metal and all those wires scared me. I didn't want him to get electrocuted after surviving the tornado. We finally did get the door up, and the ceiling had fallen on the car, but the only damage was the antenna was broken, otherwise the car was O.K.

I was just numb. There was no roof to the house, no back to the house. I was just so glad that Vernie, Carol and Becky were fine, that we were not dead. I thought, it's just a house.

CAROL HAYES

When it was all over there was a lot of confusion. The next door neighbor's dog, Brownie, was the first out because he could fit through the window well, even before my Dad broke the frame out. I remember seeing Brownie running all around the Potters' yard when I was lifted out. But what left the biggest impression was the stars. When we went down into the Miller's basement there was a horrible storm coming, but when it was over the sky was full of stars. To my five-year-old mind that just didn't make sense.

Walking across the street to our house was terrifying. Everyone kept yelling to watch out for the wires, and I could see that the roof to our house was gone, and I didn't understand where in the world it could have gone. We had a silver-maple tree in our front yard that wasn't very big, because none of the trees in Ruskin were very big, but it was our tree and now it was ruined. For some reason seeing that tree broken really upset me.

Mom wouldn't let Dad get the car out of the garage because she was afraid of the live wires and the metal garage door. So we stood around trying to figure out how to get away from there until a family drove up and asked if we needed a ride. These people were total strangers but we got in. They had a little girl and she gave me a piece of butterscotch candy. You know, that was such a simple, loving thing, and it's stayed with me all these years. I was too upset to eat it though. I held it so long the paper sweated into the candy.

PEGGY MCNAMARA

When it was all over, my brother, Mike , and I were terrified because our mother was crying, "Oh my God, I'm a widow." We knew Dad was out there someplace between our house and the Miller's and it was impossible to hope that he had survived all that. Everyone wanted out of the basement as soon as possible, but the Galler's dog, Brownie, was out first. We knew there were people on the outside helping pull all of us out the window, but we couldn't see anyone. Mom handed Shannon, who was just a year old, to a pair of hands reaching through the window. She said, "Someone please take my baby," and a man's voice said, "I'll take your baby." It was Dad.

We wandered around for a while trying to figure out what to do. I had to ride on my dad's shoulders because I didn't put my shoes on before we left the house, and now I had no shoes. Dad had escaped major injury by laying down between two houses where there was a little depression, but he had a lot of cuts and debris embedded into his skin. He didn't go to the hospital that night, but later he had to have things removed. In fact, for the rest of his life debris would work its way to the surface every now and then.

Finally we got a ride from some people who lived just west of the tornado's path. We didn't know them, but they took us back to their house where we called my grandmother. As we drove around, I kept wondering where all the houses had gone.

But the thing I worried the most about was my homework. I was in the second grade and the nun who was my teacher was so scary that all I could think of was how much trouble I would be in for losing school books.

PAUL POTTER

When we came home from Bendix we came down Craig Road to 109th, so we drove along the eastern edge of Sycamore Park. My ride kept saying, "I know it got my house," and I kept saying, "I know it didn't get mine." We ran across nails and got four flat tires, so he was driving on flats when he got to my street. He said, "Here's your street," and I said, "Where's my house?" and he said, "In hell's half acre."

* * * * *

Our shoes found, my father back from across the street, we huddled together, the Glenns of what was left of 110th Street—my family. We held each other to stop the shaking. My brother and I on the dining room table, my parents around us, we held each other to gather strength for what was ahead of us. Instinctively, my seven year old heart knew this was how we would survive.

Dad was visually shaken by what he had seen across the street. Searching through the terrific chaos of our destroyed neighborhood, he had been unable to locate our next door neighbors, the McNamaras. Horror numbed those wandering through the ruins of their homes, jumbling thoughts of anything except escape. No one was sure just where they saw them last. Pat and the kids had made it to the basement, everyone remembered seeing them there, but no, they didn't think Dick made it. Maybe they saw him afterwards, they just weren't sure. There was so much confusion. Strangers, already pouring in offering aid and transportation, needed Dad's help to load injured and homeless into cars, which sidetracked his search. It was the next day before we knew they were all right.

Dad saw our other neighbors, including Myrna Smith's husband, Jack, and knew that all had escaped serious injury. Then someone called out to him to help move Mrs. Timm, who lived directly across the street from us. She was pinned beneath a refrigerator that had fallen when a car blew up against it. Mr. Timm and their daughter, both badly injured, needed attention too. As the men moved Mrs. Timm's body to a mattress that had blown into their yard, one of them started to light a cigarette. The smell of gas was everywhere and several people yelled at him to stop. Life's precarious thread frayed many times that night.

BETTY HAMBEL

I had on a pink robe and all this blood all over the front of me. I grabbed my kids. My son had one sock on but I didn't get any clothes for him or the girls. I was too stunned. My ex-husband asked me if there was anything I wanted out of the house, so I told him my purse and a bottle of booze.

The people across the street didn't get hit as badly as we did, and they had candles, so we went over there. My oldest daughter had caught a piece of glass in her shoulder. While one of the neighbors was getting the piece of glass out, I looked up at my ex-husband and he had blood running down his face. The screen had made a "V" in his forehead and glass hit his face.

We drove out around the back way, then to Bannister west to 71 Highway. When we got to 71, cars were six deep and ambulances and fire wagons were trying to get through. We took the shoulder to try to get through to the north and my mother's. You know, I had that robe on for two days.

I couldn't believe we walked out of there with no more injury than we had. Our wounds were very minor. Our main injury was to the nervous system.

LEON FELSON

At that time, Menorah was the closest hospital to the stricken area. We realized we were getting the first wave of casualties. We started moving tables into the dining room. Within minutes, the dining room had become a sea of plasma bottles being held in the air. Personnel had come from all parts of the hospital. The central-supply supervisor appeared and the storeroom was raided. Everywhere, beds were being assembled. Beds came flowing off the elevators and we learned that patients in the hospital were giving up their beds to the injured and wheeling them onto the elevators.

Complete strangers arrived and asked to help. They were used to transporting patients to different departments. Nurses arrived from many hospitals and did yeoman jobs. I ran up to the auditorium, taking soap and blood pressure machines. By this time, doctors started appearing by the tens. The surgeons went immediately to surgery because I didn't see too many of them. The first I heard there were eight operations going on in eight operating rooms, two operations in the dining room and two in the auditorium. I don't know where the surgical technicians and nurses came from, but they were there.

A woman reported, asking where the surgical suite was. She informed the surgical supervisor that she was a surgical nurse. They assigned her to circulate in one of the operating rooms. Later, we found out she was a cab driver who had stopped her cab a block away and walked into the hospital. During the war she'd had experience as a surgical nurse, and believe me, she was a good one.

JACK BRAMS, CHIEF OF STAFF, MENORAH

There was chaos for ten or fifteen minutes, but most of our doctors had worked in the Army, and we switched over to that way of thinking. We set things up very much like a clearing station during wartime. We'd put a tag on the patient, make a quick survey of injuries, then send them to the department they needed to go.

When we drew up a disaster plan some time before this, we assumed our main problem would be help. But that wasn't the case at all. We put in a call to drug houses and within a matter of minutes we had truckloads of plasma, morphine, and tetanus antitoxin.

One of the most inspiring sights was the response for blood. We needed blood donors. We needed them badly. Someone put out the call to Rockhurst, at the time an all-male college just east of Menorah. I believe we had every young man who was sleeping at the dorm appear at the hospital to offer blood. We'd line six or eight of them up on cots and take blood, then send them off and another batch would take their place. It was quite inspiring. We got all the blood we needed.

DEAN EVANS

We sat there while the tornado went on up toward Highway 50 and Knobtown. Then I tried to drive back up Sycamore to get home, but we couldn't get very far for the debris. I finally worked my way over to Blue Ridge by dodging around corners. I went through the intersection of Blue Ridge and 110th, where the service station was, and there were high power lines and the stoplight hanging down almost to the pavement. We managed to get by, so I drove to my sister's house. Nancy was six-months pregnant and I decided to get her and our daughter out of there.

We had the radio on while we were driving in to Kansas City, and they were still talking about an airline pilot informing them there was a tornado on the ground two miles west of Grandview. They were talking about Martin City and this thing was already out of sight to the northeast.

When we got to my sister's I tried to call the paper and tell them what had happened. You'd just pick up the phone and there was nothing. Every phone in the city was busy. I drove clear down to 63rd and Paseo trying to get close enough for a phone line, but I was unsuccessful. I finally gave up and turned around and went back to my sister's. I sat there and held the phone for forty minutes and finally got a dial tone. I called the paper and they put a gal on there for rewrite and I told them what I had seen. The Associated Press picked that up. The next day I was quoted as far away as Phoenix.

Four of us tried to come back out to Ruskin. Seventy-one was jammed solid; even ambulances couldn't get by. I took them back to 63rd Street and went east clear out to Lee's Summit and came back across on Longview Road. We passed one vehicle on Longview Road and that was an ambulance. So we came into Ruskin through the back way.

One of the guys lived on the outskirts of the damage. As a matter of fact, we damaged his house more than the tornado did. He forgot his keys and we couldn't get in, so we had to kick the door in.

We got back to my house that night, but it wasn't until about one in the morning. What was horrifying as we walked up Sycamore was that I wasn't even sure which street was mine. You'd think that once I got into my house I'd go in and get my billfold for ID and cash and my car keys, but the bed was shoved up against the bedroom door so I couldn't even get into my own bedroom. All I had was a pack of cigarettes and a lighter. I used about a hundred years' luck by having that ignition open.

REV. LOREN GOINGS
I stayed up all night long. As soon as it was over I walked to my house and got a big flashlight, then headed for the A&P store. The front was all gone and the shelves and glass were laying on the floor. I went to the back where the refrigerators were all upset. There were three deaths in that store. I saw a lady who was pinned beneath a refrigerator receiving last rites. Then I went into the parking lot where a lot of people were just standing around in shock.

Later I walked the path of the tornado in Ruskin, checking on members of our church. I found a baby lying in a yard and called out in a loud voice for a doctor. Fortunately, there was one nearby.

BILL AND NORMA MARTIN
Norma: He was on the west side of the path at our friend's house. I was on the east side, and everything in between was torn up.
Bill: The bad part of walking back over to our house from the Witty's was the worry. I didn't know what I would find when I got home, or anything that had happened at that end of Ruskin. There were gas mains burning like torches, and firemen and police were screaming for people to get out because they were afraid of explosions. It took me at least thirty minutes to make a ten-minute walk. It was murder to walk through there.

Norma : I was really scared because I didn't know how he was. Of course, everybody was out in the street talking. Nobody was in their house. Our block wasn't damaged, but it was very frightening anyway.

Bill : When I did get home and saw that my family was all right and the house was O.K., I grabbed my camera and took off. Since I was staff photographer for Bendix, I felt it was my job to document the destruction because we had so many Bendix men in that area. Well, I got called some pretty bad names when people saw me with a camera taking pictures. They felt I should be helping more, I guess. I really quit after that. I didn't get many night shots for that reason. I felt kind of bad about it.

JEANNE JOHNSTON GORMAN

By the time we got to Craig Road we knew there had been a tornado. I thought we were about at my street, but I really wasn't sure because all the landmarks were gone. The friend driving me home from work said he couldn't drive into Ruskin because of the debris, so I got out and walked. I finally got to our house and it was damaged some, but not so much that we couldn't live there. Windows were broken, the garage door was sucked in and the roof was damaged. No lights were on. No one was home. My neighbors on both sides were out, and they told me my husband and kids had left before it hit. One of the neighbors said she'd take me to the fire station, which was where people were going to find one another. It was full of people. I walked in, told them my name and they said, "Your husband is dead and your kids probably are too."

Evidently, the car had been lifted up in the tornado and the boys had fallen out. When the car was dropped my husband was killed. My neighbor and I were told that kids had been taken to hospitals, so we made the rounds. You could look at kids who hadn't been identified, but not ones who had because there was so much confusion. My three year old was able to say he was "Steve," but he was thrown out of the car on another block so people thought he was a different Steve. That made him "identified," so I didn't know this until later. Craig, who was eighteen months old, really liked the name Mike, so he told the doctors his name was Mike. Some grandmother identified him as hers. Both boys were so badly cut and bruised and swollen that it was hard for anyone to tell who they were. All I could do was to go back to the fire station and wait.

The next day, the Red Cross came by and said they thought they'd found one of my boys. They took me to Menorah. There were all kinds of injured kids and no one would have recognized him. He evidently had gone thorough the car door because his face was just like pulp. The only way I could recognize him was by the top of his head. We found out later he'd gone through the air and hit a woman hard enough to break her leg. The boys were thrown out of the car in two different places a long way from where their father was found.

My sister finally found Craig at KU Medical Center. They had given him royal treatment, but of course he was quite a character anyway. He was having a good time there with the doctors and nurses, but he had horrible cuts across his face and stomach and his ear was almost cut off, but no internal injuries. After we got him home I had to take him up to the Baptist church for a nurse to dress his wounds for a while. And for years pieces of glass and wood would work their way to the surface and have to be removed from their necks and from under their arms.

E.J. AND JEAN FROUNFELTER
Jean: The entrance to the basement where we were, including the stairway down, was blocked by all kinds of debris— completely littered, just piled deep with boards and things. There were even mailboxes from other places blown into the basement. Before we went out, by crawling over everything, I asked the kids to just stand still a minute, that we were going to talk about this. "When we get upstairs," I told them, "it's going to be an absolute mess and maybe our house will be all torn up. Whatever it is, we're going to say we're thankful to be alive, let's go see about our neighbors." What else can you say?

As we were climbing up out of the debris, our dog Topper got in such a rush to get out that he knocked our daughter Marilyn down and she lost her glasses. They fell into the debris and we couldn't begin to find them.

E.J.: When we got upstairs we must have looked like a bunch of rabbits poking their heads up out of a hole. There was a truck upside down, burning, and our house wasn't there anymore. The only thing standing was our kitchen sink and the cabinet attached to it.

Jean : I said, "Girls, this is it. We made the news headlines." It was just some dumb fool thing to say, but if you can't do that, you don't survive. The house we had gone to was totally destroyed except for the kitchen pipes sticking up. We found the upholstery off the chair I had been sitting in while feeding our baby, wrapped around those pipes. Our refrigerator was out back on its side. We finally got it turned over and upright and we found two cans of beer inside. Guess what we did? We sat right down on the doorstep and drank them. There were eggs in the refrigerator too, unbroken.

CLYDE OFNER JR.

We couldn't find anybody. Driving back into the area from the service station, Uncle Bill, who had been at Pearl Harbor, said it looked like a battle zone to him. When we finally found my house it was a ghastly sight. Neither of our families were there, and all the exterior walls were gone, my 1950 Dodge slammed down into the middle of the house. There were still some neighbors around and one of them told me he thought all our kids and both of our wives had been taken to hospitals.

We found out later that no one at our house knew of a tornado until they heard it. Aunt Mabel told everyone to get into the center of the house and they put mattresses over themselves. My two boys looked out from underneath those mattresses and ended up with heads full of glass. It took us about a year to get all the glass out of their scalps. The main concern was for my wife, who was pregnant at the time. Her injuries and the trauma threw her into labor. But fortunately she was taken to Menorah, where her obstetrician was able to stop her from miscarriage. We were very lucky, but I didn't know it at the time. It took me five days to find everyone.

After Uncle Bill went off to find his family, I ended up at the Ruskin Center, where the Salvation Army set up a tent for people who had nowhere else to go. There was still a lot of rescue work going on at the A&P and the Crown drugstore. People were dug out of the wreckage all night long. The police radios were loud enough to hear as we worked clearing debris, so we started to get a sense of how widespread the damage was. Not knowing where my family was, it was a very upsetting place to be, but it was shelter. Without a car or access to a phone, I had no other choice.

JOE KRAMER

Even though I no more than got to the radio station before they turned me back to the scene, getting out there was a major problem. You had to negotiate your way through traffic that was bound toward Ruskin Heights and Hickman Mills. People, I guess you'd say, were morbidly curious, as many of us naturally are. I guess that's a legitimate human reaction. They wanted to get out and eyeball what had happened. And there was such a crowd of traffic headed toward the scene that I had to use all the influence that my marked vehicle would give me, and to do a lot of fishtailing and driving along the shoulders, to finally get there.

Then, when I did get there, it was pitch dark. I did a radio broadcast or two from that two-way radio unit in the vehicle before I even got home. And I was anxious to get home to find out how my family had fared. But I was so horrified by what I saw as I entered off of Blue Ridge and Ruskin Way. It was absolutely surreal. Of course, there was rubble and debris scattered all over, but I also remember fountains of water where fire hydrants had been sheared off. Add to that the hiss of escaping natural gas. The only light came from automobiles which had been tossed around as if they were matchbox toys. Most of them landed on their roofs and headlights and interior lights, for the most part, for some reason I never understood, were all on. Their horns had also been set off, so in addition to the spraying of water and the hissing of natural gas and the lights, you also had this eerie noise that just seemed to envelope the whole scene. It went on until the batteries were drained. It was almost a scene of desertion. It could have been totally uninhabited. There were no voices of anguish. I know there were people in there, but I didn't hear them because they were too stunned yet.

My family was O.K. My wife had taken our three little boys and had them all lie down on the floor of the clothes closet. Then, to protect them, she laid across them.

We had minimal damage to our house. Our backyard neighbors had significant damage, and the houses across the street from them were leveled to the foundation.

LEON FELSON

Suddenly I heard that none of the other hospitals were as heavily hit. We could readily transfer patients. We had just assumed that all the hospitals were getting as many emergency patients as we were. A business manager from another hospital showed up, then an administrator from another, telling us they were ready for patients. But there were no ambulances to move the patients. Those who were ambulatory we moved out in cars. It took us a while to find station-wagons, but we did. At one point, there were station- wagons lining the street, and believe me, they were a welcome sight.

SISTER MICHAELA MARIE

I was the hospital administrator at St. Joseph's. As soon as we heard of the disaster we alerted the emergency room, the blood bank and X-ray. We had wheelchairs lined up by the emergency room entrance. Outside the door, student nurses with roller carts were ready to receive patients, and we had plenty of orderlies. A lot of our doctors came in and waited in their cars near the entrance. We had a ham operator in contact with Menorah, and Father Joseph Sullivan was here to anoint the injured. But we had no patients.

HELEN EIMER

It seemed like an awful long wait. I was a staff nurse in the St. Joseph's emergency room and we were ready. Finally, they started coming in a wave for about two and a half hours. When the children came, you couldn't tell one from another because they were all covered with muck and sand. We had to put children in bathtubs to see if they even were injured. These children did not cry. There was no hysteria. I asked one little girl , who was obviously badly hurt, why she wasn't crying and she said it would seem silly.

BOB AND JEAN MCCOY

Bob: We were laying down next to the bed and had the baby underneath it. I remember I covered his mouth with my hand, because of all the insulation and stuff that was blowing around. But we didn't realize how much damage was being done until we got up out of there. That took awhile because the ceiling was laying over the bed. When we did unbury ourselves we walked out where the bedroom wall had been.

Jean: I don't think the baby ever cried. After it was all over and I picked him up he just kind of clung to me. His eyes looked like he couldn't figure out what had happened. He was just five months old. He wasn't scared. He just knew something had happened.

Bob: After it was all over, we looked out where the wall had been and there was dead silence. Then all of a sudden, people started coming up out of the debris, and I know we started checking on neighbors. Everybody was standing around, and we heard there was going to be another tornado coming, so they decided to take all the women and babies in the one car that still ran up to the high school. Paul Province, who lived a few houses down the street, was the principal of the junior high, and had a key to the high school. As we started going up the street we could see that the damage was worse than our block. I can remember going around the circle up by the Presbyterian church and people were carrying wounded. It reminded me of a bombing. We got there, but there was no school left, so we turned around and came back. Everyone was in shock and dazed.

Somebody said, "Bob, you haven't got any shoes on." So our friend, whose house wasn't as badly damaged, went back into his house and got a pair of shoes for me. I wore those shoes for two weeks, even though they were two sizes too small.

BILL AND MARY NORTHCRAFT
Mary: I didn't really know what to expect when we walked out of the basement. You know when you're first starting out and you've saved for everything? Well, we had just put up drapes, and then to see it all gone... But your second thought is, if we had still been in there we could have been gone too.

Jean (McCoy) had a Chihuahua named Susu. They couldn't find Susu after it was all over with. We came up out of the basement and Jean was there crying, "Where's Susu?" Our three-year-old son Scott tried to comfort her, saying, "Susu all right, Jean." Two or three days later they found her. She had been hiding in all the debris.

Bill: The neighbor men were going up and down the street shutting off gas. One house did explode, but I don't know why more houses didn't. You could hardly breathe for the gas fumes.

Thank goodness we had pulled our car into the garage at the last minute before it hit. Our car still worked, so we were able to drive out. There were about six lanes of traffic coming south on Blue Ridge, and we drove in the ditches and every place else trying to get out of there. We couldn't believe the people coming into the area, even people walking. Ambulances and fire trucks couldn't get through and we couldn't even find a place to make a telephone call. It was awful.

Driving out, the whole area looked like a war zone. Our neighbor, Wayne, who had been in the Pacific, said he'd never even seen anything that bad in his experience. It was worse than being in the war.

DELORES SCHUNEMEYER

From his house in Lee's Summit, my brother watched the tornado move across the horizon. He could tell it was hitting our area, so he got in his car and drove in the back way as far as he could. He had to park the car and run the last mile or so. He made pretty good time though, because by the time we came up out of the basement he was there. When he saw that we were all OK, he went back out the way he came and called our families.

Our house had a lot of damage, but it wasn't destroyed. It was twisted a little bit, but the walls and roof were still there. We had a board through the front of the house, and all the windows were broken, the screens gone, the furniture and cabinets pitted, but we could stay there. It was horrible to look at. Just a couple hours before we had been visiting with our neighbors, talking about how nice our yards looked now that the trees were starting to get bigger and everything was blooming.

BILL LEEDS

When I left work that night (as newsman at WDAF) things were comparably normal. But the minute I walked back into the newsroom after being summoned back, I realized, of course, that it was a state of emergency. Phones were ringing, loudspeakers were blaring and people were running with bulletins into the studios of both radio and television. I could sense immediately that this was going to be a big story.

The hardest part of that night was some of the phone calls. A big problem was missing persons— people looking for loved ones. I remember specifically one man who called in with an appeal for anyone who had seen his little baby girl. He said she was three and a half months old, had blond hair and blue eyes and she had been swept out of her mother's arms. The child hadn't been seen since and he was naturally, urgently, trying to find the baby's whereabouts. We put that on the air.

NORMAN CARON

I did see some looting. Police were at a disadvantage that night because we didn't have the manpower to make a lot of arrests and transport people to jail. Because I worked the south end of Kansas

City I knew local troublemakers, and when I saw these guys in the area carrying things, I made the judgment that they weren't helping anyone. Our instructions were to knock them out from under whatever they were carrying. Because of the situation, it was curbside justice.

I heard a lot of talk about cash registers from Ruskin Center being stolen. There must have been some pretty disappointed thieves, because the first thing the employees of the grocery store, dime store and drugstore did after the tornado passed was take the cash drawers to one of the stores that still had shelter. We had an armed guard there watching five of those cash drawers.

All of us were on duty until about six a.m. I remember sitting down on a big metal container and remarking to someone that I was sure thirsty. Someone said I should stand up then, because I was sitting on the pop cooler from the drugstore.

SHIRLEY GROSS

I had been told by my doctor that I needed to get to the hospital thirty minutes after going into labor because I needed a Caesarean. Here I was, more than eight months pregnant, in the basement of a badly damaged house, and I couldn't even get to my own house, let alone the hospital. When it was all over, I knew there was one thing I had to do regardless of the tornado and that was go to the bathroom. I went upstairs, picking my way carefully to avoid falling or getting cut, and there was glass embedded in the toilet seat. I used it anyway.

We got the car started, although it was pretty badly beat up, but we decided to stay there in the Schuenemeyers' basement that night. We didn't know what we'd find at home, and we figured we better save the car, particularly the tires, for an emergency trip to the hospital. We didn't get much sleep. We spent a good deal of the night preparing ourselves for what we'd find at home.

TERESA KIRSCHBAUM

I was a member of the Red Cross disaster unit, so I went out as soon as I heard about it. The police saw my uniform, let me in and told me where to go. We were set up in the garage of a house on a block where most of the houses were gone. In this house the garage was about the only part left.

I didn't see too many patients, but I sure saw a lot of frantic relatives who wanted to know what had happened to their loved ones. The only knowledge I had was what the police told me— that almost everyone was taken to Menorah, the badly injured in sta-tion- wagons. These people were absolutely hysterical. What they saw was all this devastation and they feared the worst.

* * * * *

Sitting in the backseat of our 1955 Ford, I wondered why we weren't moving very fast. Why were there so many car headlights shining on us? My throat was starting to hurt again, and I was cold. Even wrapped in a blanket I felt clammy and shaky. Would I have to go to school tomorrow? What about my teacher, Mrs. Kelly? She lived only two blocks away from us, so maybe she didn't have a house either. David seemed to be asleep in the seat next to me and my parents weren't talking much, so I looked out the window and held on to Sweet Sue.

It had taken awhile for my dad and Jack Smith to get our car out of the garage. Our other car, a 1948 Dodge, heavy as a tank, had disappeared from the driveway. Luckily, the only damage to the Ford were dents from garden tools that had blown off the garage wall. Fearful of gasoline leaks, Dad and Jack had pushed the car out of the garage before starting it. Then, after many false starts through the rat's maze of blocked streets, we drove over lawns to get to Highway 71. Now we were trying to work our way north, into Kan-sas City, to stay at an aunt's house. It was taking forever.

In a letter to relatives a week after the tornado, my dad described our family's minor miracle of the evening:

"As we were driving down Troost Avenue, I decided it was dan-gerous to continue any further without getting the windshield cleaned off. It had been covered by dust, dirt and debris so, I stopped in the driveway of a filling station to clean it off with my handkerchief and just at that moment Esther and Luana [my piano teacher aunt and my cousin] pulled up beside us in their car. They had heard the news on the radio and were so concerned about us that they had driven out as far as they could to see if they could find us. Luana just happened to look in the direction of the filling station where we were parked momentarily and shouted to her mother, 'There they are!' They were, of course, tremendously relieved to find that we were out safe and sound and we were overjoyed to see them."

JEAN HENDERSHOT

We couldn't get through on Blue Ridge, so we went in through Raytown Road, but even then there was a big tree in the road we had to drive around. But Jim was determined to get home. The destruction was completely unbelievable, but our houses weren't damaged.

My neighbor was out in the yard. I asked him if he knew anything about Hank, my husband, because I had called my mother from the auditorium to see if she had heard anything and she was frantic. She had talked to Hank just before she heard about this and he was leaving for his job. I found out later he hadn't heard about the tornado when he started out. He got up to the Presbyterian church and noticed all these people running to the church. He stopped and let them go by and wondered what they were so late to. He went on past the church and got to the intersection of Ruskin Way and Blue Ridge. All of a sudden he felt this tremendous force hit the car, and he looked up and there was this tornado cloud practically on him. Well, it scared him to death. He turned north on Blue Ridge and I bet you he was driving one hundred miles an hour. We had friends in Fairlaine, further north on Blue Ridge, who had a basement, and he felt like it chased him all the way to their house. He stayed out of the middle of that thing by only seconds.

AUSTIN SHUTE

I spent the night digging people out. I was assistant prosecutor and a deputy sheriff at the time. People needed our help, and we just started doing what we could by pulling people out of the debris and sending the injured to the fire station just north of Craig Road on Blue Ridge. We stopped anyone who came in to look around, and told them to take the injured to get help. We stopped a lot of gawkers, and if they didn't want to help we'd take their car. They didn't like it but they had to do it.

I was one of the first troops that landed in southern Japan. I have pictures of Nagasaki that look very much like what we saw that night.

MERYL OSTERGARD

I was coming home from the Optimist Club meeting, so I was one of the first into the area after it happened. There was very little damage to my house, but it took me twenty-five minutes to find that out. Once I knew my family was O.K. I changed my clothes and went out on foot to see what I could do to help. I didn't get home until dawn.

We came to one house where the only thing left was the linen closet. We heard muffled cries, opened the door, and found two children, about five and six years old, huddled in there on a shelf. They weren't injured, but they would hardly come out into our arms, they were so scared. We took them to some security people near the shopping center, but I never did know what happened to their parents.

There were injured everywhere. Even now I don't like to think of it. A tremendous amount of people just took strangers in their cars. A lot of these were pretty bloody. Now you'd worry about being sued, but people just did it because the injured needed help. Unfortunately, it was too late for some. We found dead too. We saw things you just couldn't even believe.

Major Donald Bishop of the Kansas City police radioed his dispatcher, Leo LaGrasso: "A huge knot of traffic all around the stricken area threatens to strangle operations." Bill Leeds used that information to broadcast this message over WDAF radio:

"This is an urgent appeal from the police department and the sheriff's office. Sightseers are flooding into the disaster areas and causing tremendous traffic snarls in all vital traffic arteries. This is a very important announcement. Sightseers are requested to stay out of the disaster areas. It was pointed out that emergency vehicles are trying to get victims to hospitals, and if roads are jammed, lives can be lost. So sightseers, stay away!"

GRACE KETTERMAN

We were at the Hickman Mills Clinic all night. The clinic wasn't damaged, although it was very close to the devastated part of Hickman Mills. We had plenty of supplies and auxiliary power. My husband and the other doctor in his practice, Dr. Clark, and I basically worked as a triage unit. Any cases that could not be safely handled there, we sent to Menorah or General, but we saw lots of shock and lacerations. There were also dreadful tearing and crushing injuries and, of course, all the wounds had mud and debris in them. We shaved a lot of heads that night.

I was just starting my pediatric practice, and saw mostly children that night. Generally they were brought in by a parent, but sometimes not, so people were coming in to see if they could find their children too. As a rule, the parents were more injured than the children because they had thrown themselves over their children. It's a good thing I was so busy that night, because it would have broken my heart if I'd had time to think.

GLEN AND JEAN WILLIAMS

Glen: Something hit me in the back. I had a pair of six-inch boots on, and even though they were laced up they blew off. I remember feeling relieved because they felt so heavy in that centrifugal motion that we were in. My watch blew off too. I had my boy under my left arm, and when my watch blew off something hit my arm, which ended up protecting him. Up until the last few seconds I had my daughter, but then she blew away from me. We couldn't find her at first. They finally dug her out from under the side of a house, but she didn't respond.

Jean had just gotten back from the A&P and the refrigerator was full. Of course now everything was ruined. There was some beer in there, and the neighbor that helped me out of the wreckage got into the refrigerator, which was in the backyard with the door off. He drank my beer while I was laying on the ground, unable to move. He was ornery as all get out.

Jean: I remember getting up and looking around and everything was gone. At that point, no one had started moving yet or saying anything. It was like you were the only person left on the earth. I got up and there was just bare floor. The only thing left was the bathroom stool. I lost my shoes, and both of us lost our glasses.

Glen had a punctured lung, broken ribs and a crushed wrist. People just appeared and helped. They laid him on a door and then lifted it onto the back of one of those cars with the big fins. They laid the door width wise across the fins and drove very slowly up to the high school where an ambulance took over. I was dripping blood from my wounds and I remember being worried about getting blood all over this stranger's car seat.

Our daughter, Phyllis, was taken to the old fire station on Blue Ridge, and there they sent her on to Menorah with a group of other people, so the doctors thought she belonged to that family. She was unconscious, and five, so she couldn't tell them differently.

My younger son and I went to the Independence Sanitarium with Glen in the ambulance. We had a flat tire before we got out of the area, but they fixed it and we went on. When we got to the San, the doctors were lined up waiting for patients. A bunch of nurses in starched white uniforms were there too, and I didn't want them to get near me because I was such a bloody mess. My son cut his wrist and was bruised and battered, so they took care of him right away. I had to have my leg sewed up.

You would not believe what a tornado does to your hair. It was like all the dirt in the world was shoved into your hair. You couldn't get a comb through it. It was just awful. Things came out of our skin for a long time, because if you have a puncture wound you can't get all the stuff that's pushed to the bottom. I remember the towel the nurses used to clean me up with. I was so bruised and they were using a stiff white towel that made me hurt all over.

The next morning I said to my sister, "Let's go look where they've taken the bodies to look for Phyllis." They wouldn't listen to me, so they called all the hospitals again even though we had done that the night before. Menorah said they had an unidentified girl that fit Phyllis's description. So my niece went there and it was Phyllis. She had been in X-ray when we checked before. She would look at us, but she didn't talk for two days.

You are under such a shock when this happens. You're not your normal self. Now, thinking back, I should have been a basket case, hysterical. I wasn't. Every night on TV they'd list the condition of the tornado casualties, and they'd list Glen as critical and Phyllis as critical, and it was like they were talking about somebody I didn't know. You're in such a state of shock you don't react normally at all, you just function.

TREVA WOODLING

Harry and I laid on the church ground until about two in the morning, waiting for an ambulance. When one finally came, we were told all the hospitals in Kansas City were full and we were being taken to Independence Sanitarium. All the way there I gave them names and phone numbers of our family, and by the time we got to the hospital some of my family was already there. As soon as they saw us, they headed out to other hospitals to find Diane, Dean and Denise. All that time on the church lawn and no one had seen Dean or Denise.

The doctors ruled out that I had a broken back because they set me up on the gurney and started examining me. I was in such pain. I had a dislocated shoulder shoved up under my collarbone, two broken ribs on my left side and two black eyes. I had a hole near my shoulder where they started digging roofing nails out of my back. They told me they lost count of how many they dug out of there. I thought I was going to pass out.

WALT BODINE

Once we got up to about one in the morning the bulletins began to taper off a little and we had enough people in the news room that they could keep the bulletins rolling. We were trying to get figures out how many were injured, killed, what people were doing, and where they were going. All that was coming in piece by piece.

I then went out to the scene where Randall was still set up there at the shopping center. Lighting was a real problem. Of course there was no electricity, and at first there was no light. Then some of the men from Richards-Gebaur came out with a portable generator and, along with some of the police units, they got us going.

One of the bigger stores in the shopping center, the A&P, had a collapsed roof. The store, full of evening shoppers when the tornado hit, was horribly damaged, and people were still buried in the debris.

There was still plenty going on at that time of night. The main thing I did was gather information and get ready for the next broadcast. NBC wanted hourly reports for their national news, so Randall and I split the duty. He took television and I took radio. I talked to survivors that would come by. One man came to the door of the trailer we were using, looking for a baby that was just drawn from his arms. There were terrible things going on.

The Kansas City police department received 16,983 calls that night. The next morning there were a lot of hoarse dispatchers.

LEON FELSON

We took 300 X-rays in three hours on four machines. One of our biggest problems was where to house those who didn't need to remain in the hospital but had no home to return to. Social Services showed up and, along with Red Cross, handled everyone.

BOB BABB

By the time the tornado had dissipated our job was done. We had sent out the warnings and tracked the path and that's all we could do. When I finally went home I was still pretty keyed up, so I watched television and the coverage that was being presented at that time. I didn't get to bed until about one, but I didn't sleep at all.

JOE AUDSLEY

When I got home I was still wound up, but in a sense, depressed too. All we could hope was that we did a good job. But I realized that some people had lost their lives, and I couldn't help but wish I could have done more. I was hoping our warnings had done some good, but it was too early to tell.

Hickman Mills

Front hall closet of a Ruskin home

THE HEMBREE HOME AFTER THE TORNADO.

Anna Lee Hembree's house
That fall there were postcard pictures of the disaster at the Crown Drug.

Hickman Mills looking east. Burke school is on the left.

Austin Shute's house

Hickman Mills Bank

Ruskin Shopping Center

A & P Store at Ruskin Center

YOU LAUGH TO SURVIVE

V

The capriciousness of the storm stunned a community already in shock. All through the night neighbors compared damage, astonished that whole blocks were swept away to the foundations while others were only peppered with debris. It was hard to react normally to a world turned, literally, upside down. Houses were twisted on their foundations, cars rocked on their hoods. Teenage boys found a freezer full of steaks stuck between the wheels of an overturned car. A man reported that his car had so much yard debris sticking out the windows that it looked like it had been sodded. People told of grass embedded in jagged pieces of broken glass and of straws sticking out of stripped tree limbs. A neighbor of ours told us a windowpane drove right through her closet door. The sand village we had built in our sandbox survived better than its adult neighborhood. Except where boards had fallen across one edge of the village, the houses and roads were untouched.

Anything made of cloth was vulnerable. Mothers looking for clothes to put on their bedtime-dressed children discovered insulation, glass and roofing tar throughout closets and drawers. Clothing that did survive the tornado often did not survive the washing machine. Diapers that had been drying on backyard clotheslines now fell apart on the babies, their fibers split by debris.

Frantic relatives and friends were relieved to hear ringing or busy signals when they called Ruskin homes, only to discover later that these were phantom sounds. The phones were destroyed with everything else.

The next morning brought humor along with horror. People made signs out of loose planks and doors: "MILK MAN DON'T STOP TODAY," "GONE WITH THE WIND," "HERE LIES OUR MORTAGE. One Elvis fan constructed a makeshift dummy out of tattered clothes he found in his yard and fastened the broken shell of a guitar to it. The sign read, "I'M ALL SHOOK UP." The tornado's souvenirs were easier to see in the gray morning light. Strange sculptures of debris stuck out of yards across the path of destruction, sometimes driven into the ground so deeply they had to be pulled out by machines. Many survivors had bizarre artifacts sticking out in wall or ceiling seams. Hats and other clothing items fluttered from the ceilings where roofs had lifted up and settled back down. At the northeast edge of the storm's path, all through Raytown, houses missed by the tornado's fury were the recipients of much of its trash. Fields became overnight dump sights. People awoke to find clothing and other household items decorating their trees.

The nightmare continued to scatter itself across the area, breaking up the path of people's lives. But just below the surface of the tornado's discarded pillage lay a few humorous spoils.

PETE AND DOROTHY KOTSIFAKIS

Pete: When our trees were cut down we saw amazing things. The wind must have twisted those trees, and stuff went in there and then closed up. When they started cutting we saw that there was cloth inside, right through the tree, yet the tree was not split. The guy cutting them said there was a lot of sand and debris inside them. He had to keep stopping and sharpening his chainsaw.

Across the street seemed untouched until you looked closer. There was one house that looked all right from the front, but if you looked inside you'd see there was a great big tree inside.

My brother-in-law was in the Missouri National Guard and he and another guardsman came by our house the next day. There it was, all collapsed into the basement. The other guardsman said to my brother-in-law, "Is this you sister's house?" and he told him it was. His friend said, "Boy, your sister sure is a lousy housekeeper."

A few days later my keys came back in the mail from a little town about 150 miles northeast of here. I had a little license tag on my key ring with the address on it. There was a note asking if they were mine, and the keys to all five doors to our house were there. I said to my wife, "Now if we find the doors, we've got all the keys to them."

In a little room off the dining room we had a brand new

sewing machine sitting on the floor. The floor to the entire house collapsed into the basement, but the sewing machine was still sitting in the same spot. No walls, no anything around it, but the machine was O.K. I had to crawl out on that tipped floor to get it, and it could have fallen off very easily, but I got it and it still worked.

Dorothy: At St. Catherine's Catholic Church they had clothing for people to take who were in the tornado. We lost all our clothing, so we went over there and I found a red dress of mine. Someone had found it, had it cleaned, and it was hanging there with all the other clothing for people to have. It was a dance dress, and I didn't really need a dance dress, but it was something that was mine.

MARTA SCHUMACHER

Our house collapsed into the basement too, and there was nothing left but rubble, but we found my aunt's dishes. She had a set of twelve dishes that we used just for special occasions, and she kept them up on a shelf in the closet, just set in a box, not even wrapped in anything. We found them, still in the box, out in the street. Not a single piece was broken.

When my uncle and brother made it back to our house they found the television, still plugged into the wall that wasn't connected to the house anymore, hanging upside down.

ANNA LEE HEMBREE

I have little fragile long-stemmed champagne glasses that I got as a wedding present. They were in a china cabinet that had scraped clear across the room and banged into the front door. Most everything in the cabinet was broken except for those delicate glasses. I still have them.

JUDY JONES HECKADON

Mom had her wedding rings in a case on her dresser. Our house was completely destroyed, and the dresser gone, but someone found her rings a block away. She had her initials engraved in them so they were easy to identify.

CLYDE RENKEN

We had a carton of Coke sitting by the back door in the

garage. The tornado didn't move it, but as the vacuum went by it took half of that coke out of the bottles with the caps still on. Now, people won't believe this, but it's a fact.

STANLEY JEPPESEN
I was in the Olathe Hospital afterwards, and there was an old man in there who had been blown out of his house in Edgerton, Kansas. About four or five days later word was brought to him that they found some of his stuff, a suitcase I think it was, way up north of the Missouri River.

DEAN EVANS
We had a picture on the living room wall. The picture was still there, but the frame and the glass were gone.

The tornado picked our neighbor's roof up, took the curtain off the dining room window and draped it over the interior wall, then put the roof back down. So here was this curtain hanging on both sides of the wall with no apparent sign of the roof being moved.

MARJORIE MONTEE
It destroyed our bedrooms and didn't break any glasses in our kitchen. That was so weird. We had just finished eating and were going to go before the clinic closed and I had just stacked the dishes on the counter. Not one dish was broken.

We had all kinds of strange things happen to our house. The carpet in the living room was sucked up into a point to the ceiling. It looked like a tepee. Part of our redwood fence was driven into the side of the house and it took chain links from the fence and stuck them into the house just like a pin cushion. The boy's swing set was twisted like a paper cup. It took the pillowcases off and left the pillows. We had a crucifix on the wall in the hallway. That whole wall was an absolute mess, but the crucifix was untouched.

DIANE NEHRING LEVALLEY
Our house was totally blown off the foundation. Only three things were found: my baby book and two dresses my sister and I had that were just alike.

HERB GREEN

We had this little black folder where we kept all our personal papers, including some war bonds. We went through the debris and picked up part of a wall and there it was, closed, with the strap still around it. The bonds were in there before the tornado, and no one could have gotten to them before we did because they were under a wall and we had to really dig to get to it. The folder was still latched and nothing was ripped apart, but the bonds were gone. We had to wait a year to replace them in case someone tried to cash them in and no one did. To this day I don't know what happened to them.

I remember hearing about a cash drawer from the Hickman Mills Bank turning up in a field in Lamoni, Iowa. It was intact with all the money and deposit slips still in it.

We had a six-pack of beer out in the garage and I found it out in the yard. The beer cans were not opened, the tops and the bottoms were on, but the centers were swollen out. They looked like little barrels, and they were all still in the carton. Our house was gone but the six-pack survived. I should have kept those things.

JEAN HAYES

The strangest thing I saw was a venetian blind stuck through one of our doors.

On the top of the refrigerator I had a little candy dish with a lid on it. When I got back to the house it was sitting on the dining room table, intact. No one else had been in there and nothing was disturbed. It was just removed from the refrigerator top to the dining room table.

PAUL POTTER

Both of our good coats were in the same garment bag in the closet. When it was all over, Jane's coat was hanging on a two-by-four stuck in the ground out back. My coat was laying on its back under our Chevy just like it was going to change the oil.

The house next door just peeled like an orange. Everything in the center was OK, but the walls were down. When our neighbor came back two days later he went to his dresser, lifted up the doily and picked out a couple hundred-dollar bills that he had left under there.

There were pieces of plaster floating around in the goldfish bowl, but where was the goldfish? I don't know.

We found our strong box, opened, in the backyard with six papers missing. Things like pictures, the car title and savings bonds. Those papers must have gotten caught up in the air currents because they ended up in Chillicothe in wheat stubble. A lady wrote to us and said she was out in her field and found papers with our name and address on them. It was everything we were missing from that strong box.

THELMA KIRKMAN

We had glass and pieces of wallpaper embedded in our walls. You couldn't put your hand against the wall without cutting it. We couldn't figure out where the wallpaper came from because the walls in the Ruskin houses were painted. The print was old fashioned, like you'd find in a farm house, and we learned later that it came from around Martin City. It was just amazing.

BETTY HAMBEL

When it was all over, I looked out the bedroom window and saw a car blow up. There was a flash and then the car was gone.

I saw a number of strange sights that night. My sunglasses had been on the visor of my car in the garage. We found them stuck in the ground in the backyard. This was before pantyhose, and one of the stockings I had worn that day to work was stuck up on the bedroom wall as if it had been glued there. The tornado pulled sheeting off some of my walls and laid it in the backyard with the pictures still on it. I had a love seat with a glass ashtray sitting on the arm. The love seat was knocked across the room, but the ashtray was still sitting there. One thing was very eerie. Up over the bedroom doorway something had hit and made a perfect tornado shape.

People found a sense of humor right quick. The next day we drove down the street next to ours. Even though all the houses on it were flattened, people put out signs. I remember a door laying on the ground with a dummy made out of old clothes on it. The sign said, "Here lies our mortgage." They just immediately turned to humor for an outlet.

TREVA WOODLING

In the back seat of our car were two 2x4 blunt end boards, driven right through the door. Now don't you think it would take a lot of force to break through a car door with blunt end boards?

After I got to feeling better the nurses showed me my purse. I had my black patent leather purse on my arm when I got out of the car there on the lawn of the church. Inside was a piece of sheet rock about the same size as the purse. Nothing inside had been sucked out and the purse wasn't ripped, but there was this piece of sheet rock, just sitting there. Isn't that weird?

LOUIS MANNEN

There was no sign of our divan or the other heavy furniture, but we found a ring and one crystal goblet.

JEAN WILLIAMS

Some of the inside walls were still standing in the house next to us. When they were torn down, my high school diploma was inside the wall.

BLAINE STECK

There wasn't much left of the high school office files, but what was there was peppered with roofing tar. It looked like the tornado had pulled open the file cabinet and fluttered through those files, sprinkling them with tiny pieces of debris.

AUSTIN SHUTE

There was a couple on our block sitting on their couch when the tornado hit. When the tornado passed they were still sitting there. They weren't injured, but it knocked the couch backwards.

The guy who lived behind me had a branch of a tree he cut down that he kept as a souvenir. It had an ace of spades playing card driven through it with just the ends of the card showing at each end.

BILL NORTHCRAFT

I had my paycheck on top of the refrigerator in a letter holder. After the tornado it was gone. About two or three days later, when we were taking can goods out of the cabinets on the other side of the kitchen, we found that check stuck behind some cans in the back of the cabinet.

HELEN BOYLES
I had a set of sterling silver, and even though the house was completely gone I found every piece of that silver buried in debris in our backyard.

Our minister's wife, Jeanne Collier, lost just about everything too. She was very scientific about looking for possessions. She figured out the twisting radius of the funnel and looked for her stuff at the edge of that radius. She was able to find some of their things that way.

PAT JARDES
I had my hair all in pin curls with a net over them. When the tornado floated me up to my neighbor's house, it pulled every one of those bobby pins out of my hair.

BILL AND GREG MCCARTY
Greg: Some of our bedroom walls were still standing, but the rooms were full of debris and the furniture pushed around. On one dresser there was a statue of Mary and in that bedroom it was the only item left untouched.
Bill: The closets were still there but we didn't bother about clothing that night. The next day when we came back there was still clothing in the closets, but it seemed like the good things were gone and the worn things left. I don't know how a tornado could be so selective.

E.J. AND JEAN FROUNFELTER
Jean: We had a telephone pole in the backyard that just scooted in the earth. You could stick your foot down in the trough it left. It was moved in the ground to that position. That's one of those stories people don't believe.

It was not long after Easter, and I couldn't find our baby Sally's dress. We searched and searched and finally, after about three or four days, we did find it and it had such a hole in it. I took it home, but I couldn't even keep it. Even now that memory overpowers me.

The only matching shoes any of us had were the ones on our feet at the time of the storm. No matter how hard we looked we could only find one of each pair of shoes.

E.J.: Another strange thing that happened: we had trees that couldn't have been more than two or three years old, none of them very big, but it killed all of them. They looked like they had been dead awhile. They looked like they had suffered. It literally sucked the juice right out of them.

Jean: A while later, my brother in California was looking through magazines his Boy Scout troop had collected and found a picture of our piano and an article about how people survive natural disasters like tornadoes. The point the article was making was that a sense of humor helps keep people going. Anyway, the sign said, "For sale, one slightly used piano, for sale cheap." My brother recognized our mother's piano and knew that article was about us.

People's sense of humor did get them through. I remember seeing all kinds of quickly erected signs that said things like "NO MILK TODAY, PLEASE," or "GONE WITH THE WIND." We saw one house where all that was left was the basement and the basement door. There was a sign on the door that said, "DO DROP IN." Half of our toilet was out in the yard. When a friend of ours saw it he said, "Well, you can save this for some of your half-assed neighbors."

There were plenty of strange things that happened. Our relatives kept calling and calling on the phone to see if we were OK. They said the phone just rang every time they called, so they figured our house wasn't hit, but that was crazy because our phone was on its way to Iowa. We heard some hymn books from the Presbyterian church were found in Iowa too. They took wing.

E.J.: One of our neighbors came down the next day while we were trying to clean up and said he had found one of my golf clubs. He had it all right— stuck right through his one remaining walls.

I had a sixteen-gauge shotgun that I had since I was a kid, and it was in the yard. It looked like a giant had held on to the stock and taken the barrel and just twisted it. It was not only bent down, but the sight was twisted down. I saw it, but I didn't pick it up. I should have, because the next day it was gone.

Jean: About the only thing we could salvage was our washing machine. We loaded it up the next day and took it over to some friends we were staying with to store it. Well, while we were staying there our friend's washing machine went out. We reminded them that we had a washing machine, so they plugged it in and it worked fine. So we paid our rent that way.

Sometimes we found things in the most unexpected places. I found a necklace that had belonged to my grandmother tangled up in the roots of a rosebush that had been in our backyard. Some other friends, in another part of Ruskin that wasn't hit, were going out of town for a couple of weeks, and they said we could use their house while they were gone. Now, E.J. was a sawsmith and had his hammers in our attic. Right beside the front door of these friend's house was a sawsmith hammer. How come the good Lord sent my husband's hammer to the front door of the house we were staying?

AGGIE TURNBAUGH

Back then, you understand, there weren't many young women who were reporters, especially ones driving a bright yellow convertible. Because I was a novelty I was able to get pictures others didn't.

Security around the high school was pretty tight because they were afraid the few walls still standing of the junior high building would collapse. Plus, there was a lot of looting going on. I got stopped trying to sneak in three or four times by the National Guard. Each time I talked myself out of trouble. It helps to be young. We didn't have zoom lenses in those days, so to get a good shot I had to get close. All that sweet-talking paid off when I got close enough to get a shot of the Ruskin gymnasium sign. The only remaining letters spelled, "RUIN NASIM."

*Across the street from the Northcrafts,
the sign reads, "I'm all shook up."*

Jean Frounfelter and her piano

Everything gone but the kitchen sink

Pete and Dorothy Kotsifakis pointing to the closet where they rode out the storm.

PART II

TRACKED BY THE CISCO KID

VI

Dawn spread a gray shroud of light over the scene. Those still in their homes awoke— if indeed they had slept—to a surreal landscape. Nothing was as before. Collapsed roofs buried furniture in homes where the previous day, mothers had visited over coffee. Twisted swing sets and parts of bicycles marked where children played that evening. Police and National Guardsmen watched over streets littered with the hopes and dreams of communities. The panorama of destruction, as of yet not fully realized, cast dark fingers of ruin from Williamsburg, Kansas, to Sibley, Missouri.

Although not yet known that ghastly morning, our tornado covered a path of seventy-one miles. When it hit Ruskin, it was a half mile wide, moving forward at forty-two miles per hour, with winds up to 500 miles per hour inside the funnel. Eyewitness reports by Dean Evans, Steve Underwood and Al Delugach filled the opening pages of the *Kansas City Times*. Randall Jesse produced footage for the *Today* show and Walt Bodine kept the country informed with reports on the half hour for NBC radio. All the newsrooms in town were overwhelmed with information. Claude Dorsey of KMBC left his child's piano recital to spend the night processing reports. Joe Kramer of KCMO and Charles Gray of WHB stayed in the field until they could tell their listeners what they had seen of the destroyed communities. Slowly, the scope of the story emerged.

The tornado had claimed its first lives in the small Kansas town of Spring Hill. Isham Davis and his family tried to outrun the storm in their car, but were thrown out in a field a quarter of a mile from their home. Isham, his wife Barbara, their daughters Pamela and Tamera — all were killed. Mr. and Mrs. Henry Gabbert, found in a field outside their home near Bannister and Raytown Road, were the last fatalities along the deadly path. By the end of the first day, thirty-six were confirmed dead.

The range of destruction was shocking. The Johnson County, Kansas towns of Spring Hill, Ocheltree, Stilwell, Stanley and Kenneth were all affected. With property damage over one million dollars, residents in these farming communities hardly knew where to begin rebuilding.

In Missouri, few houses or businesses along the main street of Martin City escaped damage. Eighty-five per cent of this town of 500 was destroyed. The only good news was that the tornado missed the grade school, where kindergarten graduation took place during the storm. Twenty-three of the twenty-four residents of the Ozanam Boys Home, just south of Martin City, huddled in the basement of the main house waiting out the danger. The last boy, who was in the barn milking a cow, ran to the house just in time. Although the house was only slightly damaged, the barn was destroyed. Not, however, the pail of milk which sat undisturbed under the debris.

The popular steak house Jess and Jim's, in the heart of Martin City, drew customers from all over the Kansas City area. Now there was nothing left. Miraculously, the restaurant's mascot, a parakeet named Hot Rod, still chirped inside his bent cage buried beneath the wreckage. Owner James Wright shuddered to think what would have happened if he hadn't decided to close on Monday nights just the week before.

Still traveling diagonally, the tornado clipped the northeast corner of Grandview, taking scores of houses with it. The finished portion of Truman Corners, to be dedicated that following Saturday, fell in on itself as the storm passed. Several Hickman Mills businesses along U.S. 71 were destroyed as well. Capitol Liquor Store and the soon-to-open Capitol Bowl were leveled. Crumpled cars from Debacker Chevrolet lay scattered throughout the area. The south side of the Hickman Mills Bank was completely gone. Neatly bagged groceries stood at the checkout stand of the Crest Food Center, but the windows and roof of the store were swept away. Only the oldest section of Hickman Mills was spared. The post office and the Community Christian Church, at the site of the original Hickman mill, lost only a few shingles. The tornado left souvenirs all over the city. One family at 74th and Madison, in the Waldo area, was surprised to see a woman's pink dress fall out of the sky into their yard. A man's white shirt fell at the feet of a homeowner just east of the Country Club Plaza.

After studying the debris that fell over the city, some weather bureau forecasters speculated that a larger tornado may have lifted before it hit the more heavily populated areas of Kansas City. According to the theory, the main body of this system rose as it approached the city and disintegrated at a high altitude. The roaring monster, on the ground for over seventy miles, may have been a satellite storm. Although the funnel had lifted, the small Missouri River town of Sibley felt the last effects of the storm. Roofs torn from a local service station and a church added to the debris dropped on the town.

No one disputed that Ruskin Heights received the tornado's worst fury. Some said houses toppled because they were poorly constructed. Yet the shopping center, the Presbyterian church, the new high school and the brick junior high, built like a fortress twenty years before, also lay in ruins. The fact that there were so few basements in Ruskin was pointed to again and again as poor planning. But houses collapsed into basements both in Hickman Mills and Ruskin. Everyone agreed it was a miracle the water tower held. Containing about 1,200 tons of water, making it three-fourths full, the wind swirled right through the tower's four massive stilts.

School was out for the hundreds of Consolidated District One students. Besides the high school and junior high, damage to Burke school was too severe to hold classes. Johnson school, not quite finished, had some minor damage. The twister had just missed Truman Elementary School on Bannister Road. Ruskin's graduation, scheduled for that next night, would be rescheduled minus one of the songs originally selected by the choir: "Winds Across the Sky."

Not yet quite believing what had happened, people started telling their stories to one another. A car hit the water tower, they said. Children were pulled from their parent's arms, they said. One older gentleman refused to follow his son's family to the church basement and spent his tornado moments in a rocking chair yelling, "Let her blow," and lived to tell about it. Another man, caught while taking a shower, survived unharmed but embarrassed. Father Michael Lynch remarked that he had done a lot of baptisms, but never, before this night, conditional baptisms with water from wrecked radiators. Edith Dixon had come from California for a long Mother's Day visit with her son, Merrill Woods, and his family. They were all just entering the garage when Jeanne Johnston Gorman's son, Steve Johnston, thrown from his father's car, blew into her. The rest of her visit was spent in the hospital with a badly broken leg. Stories frequently concluded with, "Unless you were there you just can't imagine what it was like." Victims, so violently torn from their neighborhoods, tended to keep in close touch with other scattered neighbors in those first unsettled days. Aches needed soothing, grief sought consolation. All these tales wove invisible threads of understanding and sympathy. Spun from disaster, they became the fabric of community.

* * * * *

A fuzz of fever and confusion surrounds my memories of those first few days after the tornado. Tonsillitis returned, leaving me disoriented and crying for my own bed. My mother was confined to bed as well. Always fighting high blood pressure, she woke up the morning of May 21 to the aftershocks of her experience the night before. My father had a hard time getting in touch with her doctor, who worked all night at Independence Sanitarium seeing storm victims. Mom knew from experience that the best thing for her to do was to stay in bed, and that's what she did. Aunt Esther had to teach piano lessons and Dad spent the day at our house sifting through debris, so David and I were taken to Aunt Betty and Uncle Dick's house.

I felt safe there. Aunt Betty assured me that my parents would join us soon and she was there to take my temperature and bring me juice. My young cousins, always good for distraction, took my mind off what I had left the night before.

While the other kids played outside, I lay on the living room couch and wondered what we would do if another tornado came. This house, fifty years old at that time, had a big basement, big enough to hold all of us and Sweet Sue too. Large trees along the curb in front almost blocked the view of houses across the street, as I was trying to block out the view I had seen out our front door. The large front porch framed by stone pillars stood in my child's mind as a fortress against any danger. I could sleep here and not awake to destruction.

By the end of the week, life seemed a little more normal. Dad and Uncle Dick had everything salvageable out of our house and stored in relative's garages and attics throughout the city.

Mom had seen her doctor, and had medicine that made her able to get out of bed. I was feeling better too, and the cut on my forehead was almost healed. Sweet Sue had to go to the "hospital" though, to get her cut fixed. I still couldn't play with the other kids yet, but I spent my days coloring with new crayons in my new coloring book. I drew funnel clouds in the large outlines in this simple book before filling them in. With my blocks I built cities on the front porch, and then knocked them down.

We had heard from the McNamaras. They were staying with their grandmother just a few blocks away and would come to visit soon. Dad had seen the Gallers, Potters and Hayes too, and there was a lot of talk all around me about building houses. Best of all, I knew Mrs. Kelly was safe. After working at our house, Dad walked the two blocks to find that the Kelly house was damaged but that she and her family were living in their basement.

We settled down into the summer making ourselves comfortable. After our baths at night, Dad read us long stories on the front porch and we counted fireflies. I had to share the bedroom with David and my two year old cousin, but that was all right, I was glad for the company. It was a summer of solace.

JOE AUDSLEY

In those days we just had highway maps to correlate funnels and the location of their touchdown points. I had a top on that thunderstorm from the radar at 52,000 feet, and a strong echo telling me where I thought the tornado had originated. So the next morning, May 21, Fred Bates and I drove down to where we thought this thing had started.

We talked to a family out in their field southwest of Williamsburg. They said they saw the tornado touch down just east of their house. We asked them at what time, because they were talking about a set-down point a half a county south of my calculations. The kids were sure they saw it drop to the ground just there, and they knew when, a little after six. We asked them how they could be so sure and they said because the *Cisco Kid* had just started.

WALT BODINE

NBC News On the Hour wanted hourly updates, so Randell

Jesse and I split up the responsibility. He took television and I took radio. From dawn until about seven o'clock that night I gathered information for these *On the Hour* national news reports. We were the lead story all day long. Mobile units were not common then, and there was nothing easy about getting that many reports out. I was feeding NBC from a pay phone in the parking lot of the shopping center. With the shopping center so devastated, it was amazing the pay phone worked.

By dawn we got word that the *Today* show wanted pictures and stories immediately. The light was still hazy, but the cameras could see through the murk better than the human eye. So Randall provided narrative, just ad libbing, while he watched the camera monitor, which could see better than he could. Right across the street from us there was a house where the only parts left of it were the two ends. The middle of the house was gone.

Some of the things we saw that first day were hard to believe, like the RUIN sign on the high school gymnasium, and sometimes it was difficult to convince the network that they weren't plants. Other things would make your heart stop. I remember seeing a child's bicycle wrapped around a light pole. While we were there the next day rescue workers found a boy in the back of the shopping center. As a reporter you are very aware people are trapped here, people are dying here, there are people who haven't been found yet who may be living or dead. Our job was to report, but also to stay out of the way of others doing their job.

All of Kansas City was unnerved. In fact, the next night or so we had a big storm scare when another severe system came up the line. Bill Leeds and I were the only ones in the newsroom and they just preempted the shows and rolled the cameras on us. We got reports off the teletype, and I stood there with a phone, talking constantly with the weather bureau, relaying what they said.

My wife called and wanted to know what she should do and I just did it all on the air. I said, "My wife is calling here wanting to know what she should do. When you hear us advising you to go to the basement, please notice that we tell our own families too."

JIM AND AGGIE TURNBAUGH
Aggie: We had our own airplane at the time. The next day

Jim and our friend, Bill Siebert, went up to take aerial photos for the *Advocate*. Jim flew a little low. I was watching from the ground with Bill's wife as they landed at State Line Airport, and we noticed a plane following them. It was the CAA, and they took his license away for a little while. He couldn't go back out and cover it anymore from the air, but we got lots of good pictures from that trip.

Jim: We were flying the path of the storm, taking lots of pictures above Hickman Mills and Ruskin. Bill had been a gunner in the war, so he was the photographer. Up there we had a unique perspective, and a necessary one, to report the scope of destruction. We got shots of the high school and surrounding area, and a good clear closeup of the car that hit the water tower, lying at the base next to the railroad tracks. But I'd have to fly low because we didn't have telephoto lenses then. About that time I turned around to tell Bill how to load another roll of film into the camera and he yelled, "Look out for that water tower!" I pulled up over the top just in time. The next thing I knew, here was a CAA plane flying right alongside me, getting my wing number.

I had been off work five weeks with a bleeding ulcer and a few days before the tornado the doctor told me I could go back to work as long as I only worked two hours a day. That Monday had been my first two-hour day back. But for the next two weeks I did nothing but work, getting all the pictures compiled into a book called *Twilight Twister.* I didn't have any more trouble with that ulcer either.

Aggie: My job the next day was to start finding people and talk to them to get the personal little stories which the *Advocate* carried. I did a lot of talking on the phone. There was not the ability to communicate then that there is now. Television cameras were too bulky and not very mobile, so the main load was up to the printed media. Jim's dad was city editor of the *Times* then. We didn't tell him anything and he didn't tell us anything.

I started working the next night with other Jaycee wives at the Community Hall in Grandview. For three days and nights we filled out identification cards which were required for anyone entering the disaster area. We were open twenty-four hours and there was a steady stream of people. I usually took the night shift because Jim was working too, so I'd take my the night shift because Jim was working too, so I'd take my boxer dog up with me. Even then it was spooky. The highway patrol came in to check on us and have a cup of coffee, and that helped a lot.

There was an eeriness in the aftermath, kind of a yellow cast to the light. Especially at night you could feel a strangeness even coming into Grandview. Nothing moved. Maybe it was still shock, but it was like everyone was holding their breath.

WILLIS WATKINS

When we went back out there the next day we saw the true extent of the damage. The garage part of our house, the part we were under in the crawl space, had no standing walls at all. We found a section eight-by-ten of someone else's house that had just come tearing through there. I'm sure that's what knocked our walls down.

It hadn't rained yet, but it was so gray and overcast that we were afraid it would and we'd lose what little we had left. We used some of that wallboard to cover what we could.

JOSEPHINE RENKEN

The worst part was working out there and sightseers going by. The next day we cleared what we could and searched for anything that we could salvage. But the sightseers just stared, as if to say, "You must be awful dumb to get caught in something like this." I felt like a monkey in a zoo.

PETE KOTSIFAKIS

The evening of the tornado I had been out working in my yard, so I had on an old pair of shoes and pants. These were things that I planned to throw away because they were so worn and didn't really fit anymore. But it was muddy outside, so I figured I'd get one more evening's work out of them and then throw them away. That's what I wore for a week.

The next day, Will Witty, a friend from Bendix, came by to see how our house was and I said, "Say, you look about the same size as me. Let me use your belt." So I wore Will's belt with my old clothes until I could get some new ones.

SIDNEY BATES

I was supposed to graduate from the eighth grade, but I

was very worried about my English grade. I hadn't done much work in my spelling book and it had to be completed for me to graduate. I was so far behind I didn't see how I would ever catch up in time. Well, the tornado blew my spelling book away.

DEAN EVANS

The next morning my brother-in-law and I went out to Grandview, where they had set up a place to get an identification card. The National Guard wasn't letting anyone into the area without one of these cards. Well, I didn't have anything to identify myself with. Everything was back in my bedroom and our bed was shoved clear up against the door, so I couldn't even get in there. They wouldn't give me a pass to get into my own home.

I finally said, "Well, what am I suppose to do?" The lady helping me asked if there was anyone there who knew me. I told her my brother-in-law was out in the car. So I brought him in and he identified himself and they let him identify me. Then they gave me a pass. I didn't have my billfold, any money, my press pass. All I had in my pocket was a pack of cigarettes and a lighter.

During that first week, my wife and daughter went to stay with her brother, but I stayed in the house, partly to protect it from looters. *The Star* told me to take all the time I needed. I bought a roll of tar-paper to cover up the holes in the roof, and a man I had known in Topeka took care of all my windows. I spent a couple days just cleaning glass and debris out of the house itself. I wanted to make sure the house was safe when my three-year-old daughter came back to it.

Right away Praver and Sons came in across the street and put a huge pile of plywood stacked up in one of the yards. About four or five nights after the tornado we had another big storm. I was in the house by myself and terrified because the storm started picking up those four-by-eight sheets of plywood and blowing them. They were crashing through the neighborhood. I thought it was another tornado.

CLYDE OFNER JR.

First off, we were all reported killed. I guess it was because some of us were missing for a few days. Anyway, my boss heard it announced on the radio. Consequently, my father-in-law went to what had been our house, put up our front door against a broken tree and wrote on it, "Any inquiries in regards to the Ofners: Happy to state all are alive."

DONNA BRAMBLE WILLIAMS

The next day we found out just how badly we all were hurt. When my dad came to the hospital he didn't even recognize Mom. The only way he knew her was by her rings. You couldn't lay a quarter on her that wouldn't hit a bruised and bloody spot. She had rocks and twigs and glass just driven right into her skin. At first she didn't know anyone. Then, when she finally was fully conscious, she looked at me and asked, "What happened to your teeth?" because both my front teeth were knocked out. I told her they were in Iowa.

I was in a body cast from my neck to the top of my legs and one arm was in traction.

My little brother had a punctured bladder and a collapsed lung. One of his legs had been almost completely severed and had a bad compound fracture. There was talk of amputating, but my dad said no one was cutting his son's leg off because he was going to play football. They were able to save it.

HELEN BOYLES

Two children who lived down the street had been up here playing with Libby and other kids that evening. Our next door neighbors told them to go home, there was a storm coming. We thought parents were there but those kids were by themselves. They were sitting on a bed watching television when it hit. Their house was pretty badly damaged, but fortunately they weren't injured. It upset all of us. We should have made sure parents were there.

There was a couple who had moved in three houses down from us just that week. They never did come back. We never saw them again.

The Saturday before the tornado I was suppose to go to a deacon's meeting at the Presbyterian church. Instead, I stayed home and did some spring house cleaning. I was working on the windows when Reverend Collier came by and asked why I didn't show up at the meeting. I told him I was trying to get the house cleaned before I started teaching Bible school and that I couldn't do everything. I don't do that anymore. I had this house completely cleaned when the tornado hit.

AUDREY GERRED BECKLEY

We came out the next day, and in the daylight could see that our house was damaged much more than we thought. But our parakeet was still alive. It was between the kitchen and the dining area, the cage covered with debris, but we could hear it and it was fine.

Immediately we rented a house in Terrace Lake, just west of Hickman Mills. Right away our Ruskin neighbors started coming over. At least once a day as many as three couples would be there, just so we could all be together.

A few days after the tornado, some friends of ours came over to the house we rented and asked if they could come see our Ruskin house. Even though there was very little left, to them it was our house, so they came to get us first before looking at it.

When we got there a bunch of people were walking through, and one little girl evidently spotted a doll and she picked it up. I walked in and said, "I'm not a very good housekeeper, am I?" Boy, they started dropping things.

LOU DAVIS

My real estate office, just north of the Hickman Mills Bank, wasn't damaged. When I got back the next day people started congregating there. Tom Owen, another Ruskin salesman, and I were the only ones who really knew the area block by block, and the people who lived there. We had a big map we used, but in many cases we didn't need it.

The Red Cross started getting messages for people from all over the country. But how are you going to deliver messages when there are no addresses? So our American Legion post set up a message-center and I became the message center chief because that's what I did in the army. We set up headquarters at the Ruskin Baptist church and our legionnaire boys delivered messages. The map told the boys where the houses should be, but some were there and some weren't. Even knowing the area it was very hard to find people. The Red Cross gave us a jeep to use with a portable radio in it to keep in touch with the office so that when they'd get communications they could check our information. Finally, someone took my map.

Sometimes we got lucky finding people. I remember having a message for someone I knew in Ruskin and looking out the window to see him walk by. I yelled out to him and he got his message.

TREVA WOODLING

We all ended up in different hospitals. We don't know who found Dean, or where, but he was taken to General Hospital. He was bruised all over. The doctor said you couldn't put your finger down on him without hitting a bruise. He was two years old, and scared, and cried quite a bit, so the nurses just carried him.

Relatives found Denise in a Raytown morgue. We never found out where she was found, or who took her there, but evidently she had been hit in the head and died instantly.

Diane was taken to Menorah and had both her legs in traction. She was almost five, and so embarrassed to be laying there in a diaper. She just hated it. Mr. and Mrs. Violet, these dear friends who lived next to Harry's mother, found out about us being in the tornado and they went over every day to stay with Diane because she was just petrified. She would hold on to their hands so tight because she didn't want them to leave before she fell asleep. So they'd wait.

Our house was badly damaged, but if we'd stayed at home it would have depended on where we were as to whether we'd be injured or not. The people who came to clean up said we had enough lumber and light fixtures in our living room alone to build another house.

I had worked so hard getting ready for my sister's shower. I painted the whole inside and reupholstered two chairs. I found out materialistic things don't mean anything. Everything can be taken away just like that — even life.

CHARLIE COOK

The next day my brother-in-law and I went to look for his secretary who lived in Ruskin right behind the high school. Her house was gone and there was no sign of anyone around. There was a basement, though, and we thought maybe she and her family were staying there. We started to investigate, and a guy followed us down the basement stairs with a gun pointed at us. We told him who we were looking for, but he didn't seemed convinced. That scared me more than all the National Guard and their rifles. This guy wasn't trained to be controlled. He was upset and protecting what little he had left. We got out of there in a hurry.

DIANE NEHRING LEVALLEY

The next morning my dad found me. He had been unable to get into the area by car because of all the traffic, so he walked. When he got to what was left of our house, he was frantic because there was no sign of us. He made the rounds of the hospitals and found my sister at St. Mary's with a skull fracture, concussion, and covered with long deep cuts. Her head was bandaged, her eyes swollen and her whole body black and blue. She was in the hospital for a long time.

My mother was a small women, and at first she was being identified as a teenager, so it took awhile for dad to find her. When he picked me up he couldn't even tell me she was dead. He had my aunt tell me. When my sister got out of the hospital it was the same thing again. He had waited all that time and hadn't told her yet. I remember exactly where we were and what he said to her. It was like Mom had died all over again.

We had just moved to Ruskin from Grandview and I was finishing out my fourth grade year there. I wanted to go back to school right away, but my dad wouldn't let me. I guess he thought it would be better for me to stay with my aunt and uncle, but I needed to be around my friends and in a normal situation. I couldn't talk to my dad about Mom at all, and my grandmother and aunt were just as private as he was about feelings. My sister was younger and so badly hurt that she needed a lot of attention, so I really had nowhere to turn. That's why it hurt so much not to go back to school. I had nightmares for years about my mother's death. But I learned to accept it, and just kind of handled it on my own.

JEAN HAYES

The next day when we came out, Vernie went over to talk to our next door neighbor, Milt Galler. His wife, Annabelle, was in the shell of their house smashing the few remaining glasses, she was so upset. I think it was pure frustration.

CAROL HAYES

I remember coming out in the daylight and seeing it all for the first time. Of course what affected me the most was seeing all my ruined toys. My toy giraffe had a broken neck and my favorite bear, Corky, had to be thrown away because he was full of insulation.

Mom had let me plant some tulip bulbs by the back step, and I dug all over looking for those tulip bulbs. It just broke my heart that they were gone.

DANA GALLER CORDER

Mom heard on the news that there was an unidentified little girl in the hospital who kept calling for Coco. The nurses would bring her hot chocolate but she'd still call for Coco. Well, Mom knew that the little girl across the street, the one whose mother died, had a dog named Coco, so she went to the hospital and identified her.

MIKE MCNAMARA

I went out to the house with my dad the next day. I was only five, and felt very big to be allowed to go with Dad. After we inspected the house we stood in the front yard and I'm sure Dad felt helpless. He picked up a piece of debris and handed me a smaller one. Then he threw his at one of the remaining windows and without a word I did the same. We stood there, father and son, throwing things at our house, and I felt a closeness to him that I've never forgotten.

BLAINE STECK

Early the next morning I went back over to the high school to start shifting through the rubble. When I got there the rescue workers were still looking for our janitor, Mr. Kildow. I hoped somehow he'd gotten out. He had a son graduating from Ruskin that year that he was so proud of. Not long after I got there he was found under debris very near to where they found our nurse, Mrs. Guyll, the night before. They were killed by the same collapsed section of ceiling.

BILL EAGER

I was really worried about my football shoes. They were in my locker in the junior high building, and I was afraid they were going to charge me for the shoes and my books. So the next day I went across the street to the school, sneaked past the guards, and got in. My locker was all bent up, but I finally got it opened and the shoes were all right.

RUSS MILLIN

I was on the school board at the time, and we had just hired a new superintendent, Carl Wagner, that previous January. The day after the tornado he got to work letting contractors clean up the school property, and even lined contractors up to rebuild. Well, we were going to have to use federal disaster relief, and when the government gives you money you have to let everything out for bid. Dr. Wagner was thinking of the district's best interest, and he knew we'd have to work hard to get things ready for fall classes, but in his eagerness he caused a little problem.

GENE MONTEE

I was working for Allstate at the time, and I called my boss from Union Station before we left for Pittsburgh. He immediately sent out a security guard to watch our property. There was a lot of looting even with the National Guard there, but we didn't have any problem, thanks to the security guard.

I came back up the next day with two of my uncles to go through our possessions. We had everything ready to move into our new Olathe home by the 27th, which is when Marjorie and the boys joined me. Moving certainly was different than I had anticipated.

THELMA KIRKMAN

We had a bird named Echo who blew out the dining room window. We looked and looked and couldn't find him anywhere. Finally the Salvation Army put an ad on the radio that we were looking for our bird, Echo, and that he was friendly and could talk. Someone in Ruskin Hills called the radio station and said she was hanging up her clothes on the line about three days after the tornado and a bird came down and landed on her shoulder. They got a cage and kept it. She said we could come over and look at him. When we got there, right away Echo said, "Give me a kiss." The lady said, "Well, he's your bird," but the family's children had grown so attached to him that Roy went out and bought them another bird. So we got our Echo back.

CHARLES GRAY

Even though I was out there most the night, I really didn't have an idea of the scope of devastation. You had to fly over the scene to fully comprehend it.

We did follow up reports for a couple of days. By then, it became apparent that residents felt put upon by all the extra people around. As a newsman, I wanted to tell their story and help them, not create an imposition.

Much later I went to some disaster seminars, and one of the things talked about was how important it is for the mental health of disaster victims to clear away the debris as soon as possible. That's what those residents were trying to do, and after a while we were just in their way.

BETTY HAMBEL

The people behind us had pulled out a mattress into their front yard and were putting things they could salvage on it. While they were digging things out, someone came by and stole it.

HERB GREEN

We settled with our insurance company within three days. But they made it clear that anything left on the property after then belonged to them. So we had to have anything salvageable, which was next to nothing, off the property before then. They said they'd clean it off and haul stuff away, or we could do it and they'd allow us $500. Even though our foundation was wiped clean, I wanted to go through the debris to make sure we found what we could, so we did that. But that meant we had to do it quickly.

I had pulled out our tub and sink because you could sell them at a junkyard. I worked and worked to get them out to the curb. The next day I came out and someone had taken them.

JEAN FROUNFELTER

We had to be stalwart. We hadn't lived in Missouri very long and we had no family here to lean on. We were only close to neighbors who were in the same situation we were, and some church friends. We leaned on our friends, and believe me, they were friends. Very quickly we learned they were true friends and we tried hard not to abuse that.

The next morning I knew I had to give my girls a job that would make them feel important and not sorry for themselves. I put them in charge of cutting out all the articles in the paper about the tornado. For days they kept their scissors handy both day and night. We had quite a scrapbook.

We spent the next day going through debris on our property. We saved one kitchen cabinet. I had some everyday plates in there, and some silverware in the connecting drawer. We took the cabinet down so we could lay things in it that we'd find. When we came back later it had been taken. Someone had relieved us of it.

JEAN HENDERSHOT

We got all the books out of our library before it rained the next day. That was a real blessing. It was kind of strange what happened in there. The library was just a couple doors down from the Ben Franklin store, and severely damaged, but the roof blew down at an angle so that it covered about half of our space. All the books that were under the roof were perfectly fine. The ones on the other side had splinters, rocks, tar and insulation just blown right into them.

AUSTIN SHUTE

I set up a temporary office in a trailer someone put up out near the entrance to Ruskin, in front of the high school. I was president of the Homes Association at the time, so people had questions for me in that capacity. But I was also assistant county prosecutor, and this office was so people would have someplace to go to with complaints or questions on how to handle the problem of looting. That's about all I did for a month. It had to be done.

I had gotten permission from my boss in the prosecutor's office to set up this adjunct office out there. Well, then I guess he thought I was upstaging him politically and changed his mind. So I said fine, I'd do it on my own and I took the prosecutor's sign down. If I hadn't provided this service someone would have, but these were my neighbors who needed help.

SHIRLEY GROSS

We were told that night in the Schuenemeyers' basement that more than likely our house was gone. We got up the next morning and walked over there, prepared to find it destroyed. When we found it was still standing there, everything in it, that was fantastic. We'd already dealt with the fact that it might all be gone.

Our next concern was for some very good friends of ours who lived down the street from the Presbyterian church. From what people told us, they appeared to be right in the worst part of the path. We walked over there and were shocked. Nothing was there, only a cement slab, but no walls or sign of their things. No one could tell us for sure where our friends were, but they thought we should try the hospitals. The wife was pregnant too, and we were very concerned. All of them were at Menorah and their little girl was severely injured. It was an agonizing time.

JOE KRAMER

I was on the scene for thirty-six hours. I checked on my family and then went back and reported one story after the other on the two-way radio, from what we called the news cruiser. That was a station-wagon with a two-way radio in it and KCMO News printed on the side. The area looked like it had been bombed, and we were working in battlefield-like conditions. Right away, Austin Shute set up an office and did a great deal to get people calmed down. The fact that he started organizing recovery efforts the next day showed people they could survive this tragedy. We needed someone to take charge.

As a news person I was asked to verify the names of the fatalities. In doing that I went to the George Funeral Home in Grandview that next morning. As I walked in to talk to someone about a list of people, I realized this was not really a funeral home at the moment, but a morgue. Every door I opened, every corner I turned, there were dead people. Some were lying on couches, some on the floor, all in perfect neatness. They had been treated with great respect, but the funeral home was completely over-whelmed with fatalities from the twister. I didn't recognize any of them. I didn't notice that any of them seemed brutally injured.

I heard a lot of stories that first day and a half, but one I particu-larly remember. I believe it to be a true story. There were National Guard barricades to keep those out of the area who had no legiti-mate reason to be there. A distinguished older gentleman came driving up Grandview Road. He was stopped by a Missouri National Guard private, armed, manning a barricade. The guards-man looked into the car and saw that the driver was Harry S. Truman. He told Mr. Truman he couldn't let him through because he didn't live there and he didn't have a pass. The guardsman became quite upset that this should be happening to him, that he would have to deny passage to the former President. Truman said, "Young man, do you have a two-way radio?" and the guards-man said, yes sir, he did. Truman went on: "Call your command post and tell your commanding officer that his former commander-in-chief would like to be passed through the line here so he could drive up the road to visit his brother's home." So the kid did.

BILL MARTIN

There was a fellow who had worked for me in the photo lab at Bendix who had moved. But he was in town that next day and called me at work to make sure my family and I were all right. He said he was sure worried about us. We didn't know until later that he hadn't been able to get a hold of his mother. She didn't live in the damaged area, but she and a friend had taken a ride out to the Richards-Gebaur area. Days later the airbase still had two unidentified bodies. Lo and behold, it turned out to be his mother and her friend.

REV. LOREN GOINGS

I didn't know until the next morning how extensive the damage was. As soon as it was light enough, I visited all of our church members who were in the path. Some of them still had walls standing and partial damage, but others had nothing left at all. Everything was completely gone. One of our members already had a little trailer and everything he owned was in there. It was pitifully small. Our own house didn't appear to be damaged, but it was shook so badly that all the nails that held the sheet rock were popped. You could see where they were. We had to have the whole house renailed and repainted.

There was an awful lot of curiosity about what our community looked like. The National Guard could keep sightseers from coming in, but there was nothing that could be done from the air. The commercial air flights for several days circled and let people see the damage. I don't know how many planes did that, but it was a lot.

JOE NESBIT

There was another week of school scheduled, but of course classes were dismissed for the year for the whole district. We asked teachers to finish up their report cards and we mailed them to the students.

According to the insurance company, Burke was thirty-five percent destroyed. The upper wing, closest to the railroad tracks, was practically gone. It blew the walls down and blew part of the roof off the all-purpose room. The center wing was still standing but had damage to the roof and broken windows. The lower wing, or the west side, had mostly debris blown in and broken windows. Fortunately, all the enrollment cards were in a safe in my office and they were all right.

JEAN MCCOY

It didn't rain that night, which was a miracle. That could have destroyed anything that was left. The next day we were wondering what we were going to do to get the stuff out of the house. A friend came by with a truck and asked if we needed any help. He was a hero to us. That saved us. We were able to take what was left to the Northcraft's garage.

We salvaged our refrigerator and washer and stored them there. While we were at work, someone came by and took not only our washer, but the Northcraft's too. Neighbors saw the looters loading them up, but thought it was some men we had asked to move the washers for us.

MARY NORTHCRAFT

The men of the neighborhood really tried to protect our property, but we had things stolen anyway. Before the National Guard got there, our next door neighbor was on the corner with his shotgun, and at the top of the block another neighbor had his. They were just daring anyone to come through.

Both the McCoy's and our washers were stolen right out of our garage at eight o'clock in the morning. It was so hard to tell who was helping and who was stealing because so many people were bringing trucks in to haul stuff out. But we were gone, and the neighbors didn't know, so we lost our washers.

I guess they were going to take a clock of ours too, because it was sitting by the front door. The police took it to try to get fingerprints, but we never got it back from them.

GLEN WILLIAMS

I was in the hospital for two weeks. I had crushed bones in my arm, and I was in a cast forever and off work for seven months. But after that, I never had any trouble with that arm. I also had broken ribs, and I could hear them rubbing together when I moved.

My father-in-law was a real joker. Someone took a picture of our house swept clean except for the toilet, and brought it in to show me in the hospital. He looked at me and said, "Next time you're in a tornado, just put your head in the toilet."

Ruskin Junior High

New Ruskin High School gymnasium

Sycamore Park debris pit

Martha Frounfelter at Burke school

Our house
My bed was on
the other side of
the dark area.

The McNamara's car

My dad's car was
found two blocks
away.

Frounfelter's house

Jean McCoy in her kitchen

WHEN FORD SHAKES HANDS WITH CHEVY

VII

In the May 23, 1957 edition of the *Jackson County Advocate*, there is a full page advertisement showing the hands of two men grasped in a handshake. It's captioned, "Here's cooperation. In an effort to continue business as usual in this stricken area, effective immediately Town and Country Ford will move to [new Grandview location] and Debacker Chevrolet will move to the former Town and County Ford building." Cooperation became a key word that summer.

By the time Governor James T. Blair Jr. declared martial law and called out the National Guard on the night of the 20th, help had already arrived, orders of Mayor Bartle. Kansas City police and fire fighters were already on the scene. Grandview police and the fire department arrived in Hickman Mills just minutes after the storm. Southwestern Bell set up emergency communication centers for the National Guard at four stations throughout the damaged area. With all utilities out, the Kansas City Power and Light company had line crews in the area immediately. The Missouri Public Service Company and the Gas Service Company worked all night to shut off gas mains. The 110th Engineers Army Reserve arrived from Richards-Gebaur and provided the area with much needed searchlights. The Jackson County Health Department set about the task of protecting the public from damaged food from affected grocery stores and restaurants. The Salvation Army arrived within ninety minutes after the funnel. The Red Cross had an office set up in time to serve morning coffee. By lunchtime, they were ready to serve three hundred sandwiches and thirty dozen hard-boiled eggs.

Complacency blew away with everything else, exposing generosity and compassion. The Parke Davis drug company offered to replace any destroyed medication at no charge. Salyers Prescription Shop in Grandview offered free delivery. Rainen Furniture set up a four-point plan to help victims get back on their feet. Any of their present stock of used furniture was given to tornado victims. They offered their store space as a clearinghouse for all people who wanted to donate furniture. Anyone wanting new furniture would have payments deferred for six months. All present balances of destroyed furniture were canceled. The Brookside Merchant's Association set up a clothes collection center at one of their stores. Milgram's grocery store stood behind its slogan of "Hi Neighbor": the stores worked in conjunction with the Red Cross and set up clothing collection sites.

Allstate, Farmer's Insurance, and Pacific Mutual placed notices in the local papers informing their clients of extra services, such as delayed premium payments and extended hours for claims adjustments. Many cleaners throughout the metropolitan area offered to clean any clothing surviving the tornado at no charge. The Grandview Bank volunteered its staff for free legal advice and allowed anyone who needed a safety-deposit box to use theirs free. Because of the large number of businesses affected by the storm, the merchants of Kansas City and outlying areas rallied to the needs of the stricken communities.

The hearts of countless others were opened. One little girl, hearing that a girl her age had lost all her toys, sent her favorite doll to comfort the child. A benefit luncheon set up by the University Women's Club raised disaster-relief funds. The Bruce School, a private institution for children, opened its facilities to the children of victims who needed day care. Many high school seniors from other schools donated money to the Ruskin High School Fund. Bishop Hogan seniors had collected money for a thank-you breakfast for their parents, but instead turned it over to the senior class of Ruskin. Movie theater owners in Kansas City donated to the Red Cross, the proceeds of two nights. Proceeds from a local beauty contest were added to the relief fund as well.

As the country learned of the disaster, aid poured in. A Girl Scout troop in Denver, touched by the homelessness of their fellow Girl Scouts, worked for a month doing odd jobs around their homes and neighborhoods. These fifth graders dug dandelions, washed windows, caddied and baby-sit. At the end of the month had collected $17.69. They mailed it to the president of the Ruskin Homes Association with a note stating they wished it to go to a family of a Girl Scout.

With the approval of Jackson County's most famous son, the money raised at a Democratic dinner the night after the tornado was donated to a relief agency to assist families in the disaster area. Harry Truman spoke to 600 guests at the Hotel Muehlebach. The topic was the United Nations, but his opening remarks were on his old neighborhood. "It is a sad situation in southern Jackson County," he said. "That is home to me. Some of the devastation was on a farm where I pitched many a bundle of wheat."

Severed from their normal daily patterns and, in some cases, their past lives, the tornado victims lost connections. Many of these were forever lost, others regained and strengthened. But because of the response of those touched by the victims, new connections formed. Small in their simplicity, they were giant in their importance.

JIM AND AGGIE TURNBAUGH

Aggie: Monsignor Ruysser got me to go out in the Red Cross mobile canteen. We drove up and down the streets offering coffee, sandwiches, snacks. After the first day or so it was primarily workers we took care of. I was surprised there were so few people who came up to us.

For a totally unorganized, unprepared area, they got organized in a hurry. Grandview was still standing and had working phone lines, so it bore a lot of the load of helping.

Jim: The Mennonites moved in very quickly and strongly. They'd come and start raking people's yards, trying to glue people's lives back together again. They were among the few organizations that came in to do actual physical labor. Whatever people needed they wanted to do.

The Jaycees could immediately see that someone was going to have a need for emergency funds and the Red Cross would be bled white because of the size of the storm damage. So as soon as the bulldozers cleared off Highway 71, we got together a boot block type of operation and just asked people who were coming through to contribute. My God, the money just poured in. We collected around $13,000.

The Highway Patrol came down and stopped us and said we couldn't be holding up traffic like that. We thought about what we could do, and decided to call the president of the Missouri Jaycees, Tom Eagleton, and ask him what to do. He said he'd take care of it. So he called his father, who happened to be Missouri Attorney General at the time. His father said he'd call back. Within a half hour Tom called us back and said, 'Go ahead, we've got the Patrol problem solved."

STANLEY JEPPESEN

I was at the Olathe Community Hospital. When I got home, I received a bill for everything remaining after insurance paid. It was between $300 and $600. The hospital sent that bill as they would to any patient, just in normal course. About two days later I got a copy of the same bill, marked "paid." The hospital had called a board meeting and decided if there was any cost that the tornado victim had to pay, they would erase it. That affected eight or nine of us.

GEORGE MOORE

I worked at Westinghouse and they let me take off work to help out in the Ruskin area. I ended up at the Baptist church helping the Red Cross with claim forms. I also took food between their office and Martin City.

I also helped with the clothing donations at St. Catherine's Catholic Church. We set up racks and tables in the basement of the church, and had so much clothing donated we ended up taking care of an awful lot of people.

ELINOR STEINBRUECK

My college sorority gave me a surprise party after the tornado. They called it a "This Is Your Life" party. It was really nice, and besides giving us some cash to work with, it really made me feel taken care of.

PETE KOTSIFAKIS

The very first help is the most important, no matter how much it is. The Salvation Army gave us money for underwear and Bendix gave us money. Right away, a box of clothes my mother-in-law had collected from her neighborhood came. We took what we needed from it, although it seemed like we hardly made a dent in it, and then passed it on to others. It was this first help that got us back on our feet.

Twenty or thirty men came over from my department at Bendix and helped clean up our lot. They all made a line across the yard, each one with a rake, and went to work. That was so impressive. At least they got all the junk out of the yard so I could see that there was ground under there, that it was our place.

The Mennonites came around and asked if we needed help, but since we did have help I told them other people needed them worse than we did.

A guy I had worked with before I worked at Bendix had a truck and he came to help me move stuff. Another man I had worked with asked me if all my clothes were gone. I told them they were. So he went to friends of his, who were pretty well-to-do, and said he knew people who needed their suits more than they did, and brought me back some.

Sears was great to us too. We had just bought a stove from them and were making payments on it. Sears said, "Tell you what, we'll just give you another to replace yours."

KEN MARLEY

I was at the National Guard headquarters the night of the tornado, doing drills. We were aware of the tornado from radio reports, but we had to wait for the governor to give the go-ahead. The trucks were in Raytown and had to be loaded at the downtown Kansas City headquarters, but we still made it out there by ten o'clock.

I pulled guard duty. That meant we were to search the area for victims, guard certain areas and restrict entrance. I ended up being out there eight days and nights. We slept in tents, rotating shifts. Most of the time I was to guard the drugstore on Highway 71 and the Hickman Mills Bank.

The area was blocked off, but a couple nights later three young men drove up in an old furniture truck with the printing missing. This was very early in the morning. They said they were there to "pick up a few things." That's what we were afraid of. They must have thought I was the only one there. When my partner cocked his rifle, they changed their minds.

We really didn't meet any resistance or have serious confrontations with anyone. The sightseers were the worst. There were a few instances on Highway 71 where rifle butts were banged into cars.

CLYDE RENKEN

A bunch of men came walking through the area and wanted to know if we could use some help. I said, "Well, yes, I can use some help," but I thought they were looking for paid work. Turns out these fellows were Mennonites. They came and wouldn't take any money. They closed up their businesses or whatever they were doing and said you need help, we'll come and help you. They helped us for a couple of days and said all they wanted was a picture of the house when it was finished.

Bendix was real nice too. They told me if I showed up for work they'd tell me to get back out there and take care of my business. The Bendix company, along with the workers, made up a pool of money. Everyone who had damage got some of this money. In fact, they came out the next day with some, and we got the rest later.

REV. LOREN GOINGS

The Red Cross came in and set up in the church— just came in. There were hundreds, maybe even thousands, of Red Cross meals served out of our kitchen. I don't know who all came to eat. It may have been people whose homes were destroyed, or just couldn't cook, because there was no gas or electricity for a while. But they came by the hundreds. I do know the Mennonites ate at our church. Boy, they were workers. The Red Cross brought tables for the dining area and tables for the office work. They were there six weeks. When they left, they left the tables with us. As they were leaving, their leader came to me and said, "I realize we didn't ask permission to use your church," and I told him "Well, you've got it." The Red Cross was amazing.

Besides feeding people, the Red Cross office there decided how much aid to give people. I was on their committee of eight. There was one labor union representative from in town on the committee, but most everyone was from the area. We'd get a request, then see what damage was done. The leader would estimate how much money to give that family. I don't remember turning down a single request.

Someone from Rival Manufacturing came out and said they wanted to look at ten houses and give one thousand dollars to each family. I didn't want the responsibility of selecting these homes myself so we got a committee of three and went out to pick the ten.

There were two or three people who set up in the basement who had short wave radios. The telephones were all gone so they were contacting people on the outside who would call in looking for friends or relatives. They helped greatly and were there for several days.

ALICE HONS

I headed up the health and welfare inquiries for the Red Cross at the Ruskin Baptist Church. I went out there the next morning and set up the office so we could start locating people. In that first two weeks we had 9,000 calls. And of course you couldn't just drive over to the person's house, because the roads were blocked off in many cases and usually the people were no longer there anyway. Our volunteers surveyed the damage, talked to everyone they could, and urged them to call relatives and contact others who might be trying to call in.

So many times when we explained our services, people would tell us they had never asked for help before and they were reluctant to now. We tried to make it clear this was not charity, but neighbors helping neighbors.

HOWARD MASSEY

I was the assistant fire chief in Raytown. We knew there was a tornado in the area, we could see it in the air, and we were in communication with other departments. As soon as we lost contact with the Hickman Mills fire department we made a mad dash. First we went to Bannister and Raytown Road where a service station was destroyed. When we got to Bannister and Blue Ridge we couldn't even get through with our fire truck. This was before the National Guard cleared a path.

It was three days and two nights later before I got home. We had loudspeakers on the trucks and fire-chief cars, telling people not to light matches, and we didn't have to put out one fire.

We pulled a lot of people out from under debris, but the most horrifying sight was on the catwalk of the water tower, where we found a baby lying dead.

Most of the time we were so busy we didn't have time to look around except at what we were doing. We slept when we could, which wasn't much, but managed to get a few hours each night at the fire station on Blue Ridge. Construction crews came to help, along with the National Guard, and it was surprising how well we all worked together. We were there for the same purpose, and no one was looking for glory.

THELMA KIRKMAN

The Salvation Army had a group out here. They'd have two people walking in pairs covering this area, contacting everybody that they could. They wanted to know what they could do to help. When they asked us if we needed anything, Roy said he couldn't think of anything, that there were people worse off than we were. But we thought it was so nice. Afterwards they gave us a starter set of dishes. They did a lot of good out here.

JEANNE JOHNSTON GORMAN

There were nurses up at the Baptist church, and I had to

take Craig up there to get his arm dressed after he came home from the hospital. The Red Cross was wonderful. They were the ones who took me to find my sons the day after the tornado. I didn't know what kind of money I'd have. They paid my bills that summer until I got an insurance settlement. They were just fantastic. They sent my kids a Santa Claus that Christmas. I still have it.

PAUL POTTER

We'd be out here working and people would come by with sandwiches. One time this lady came up with meatloaf sandwiches. She'd made them herself and they were good. People would come up and do that kind of stuff, anything to help.

Our best friend was the National Guard. They came in and kept the looters out and let us get in and start cleaning up. We all had to have identification cards and we had to have them with us because the National Guard wasn't about to let anyone in.

Sears was wonderful too. They said they were going to put everything back in the house that we had financed from them. They even gave us dishes and silverware.

When I went back to work, a man came up to me and asked if I was Paul Potter. I said, yes, I was three days ago, but I wasn't sure who I was then. Reality had begun to hit me. The guy said, "Well, if you're Paul Potter, we've got something for you." He handed me an envelope with a check in it, shook my hand and wished me good luck.

A gentleman from our church had me come into Rothchild's, and he had me get a tie, underwear, suit, shoes and socks. The people he worked with gave him money to do that for me. Kansas City has always had a big heart.

BETTY HAMBEL

I went up to the Salvation Army tent and looked around. The lady in charge said take whatever you need. I told her I really didn't need anything, that none of our clothes were gone. She insisted I take clothes for the kids and blankets because, she said, "What money you have you're going to have to use for something else." I'm still using those blankets.

HERB GREEN

We got a house to stay in that summer through the Red Cross. A lady had called them and said she had a little house in back of her house. It had been servant quarters at one time, and if a young family needed a place to stay they could use it free. We stayed there three months, until our house was ready to move back into.

Our house was across the street from Sycamore Park, and I remember going out there and seeing the Mennonites. They set up two tents there in the park, one for sleeping and one for cooking. No women came, but about fifty men showed up from all over.

LUCILLE MOTSINGER

I was a Red Cross nurse's aid and I got a call at five the morning after the tornado to go out to the disaster area. We met at the Red Cross office downtown and drove out in a convoy. I had to wear a uniform, and I remember it was hot and sticky and very dirty because of all the debris. We had a big canteen tent set up where we served cold drinks, coffee and sandwiches. We also had a mobile canteen in the back of a pickup truck so we could serve people who were working at their home. I spent the day roaming around in that truck. As soon as we ran out of food we'd go back to the main tent and there would be more. We gave an awful lot of food away.

MARJORIE LANGFORD

I always thought it was interesting that Mayor H. Roe Bartle was criticized for a lot of legal things he did, but he was never criticized for the illegal thing he did in sending Kansas City police and firemen outside city limits. He was more concerned in doing the right thing and he knew we needed his help.

We had lots of help as the summer went on. My husband contacted Menorah to pay whatever we owed. There was no charge. I guess they didn't even try to keep records for all those services.

My husband taught at Southeast High School at the time. A huge crew of seniors came out one day and combed our seven acres. They went over it step by step, trying to salvage anything they could.

We had a lot of rare birds, with runs for them. Of course many of them were killed. When the Mennonites came, they tried to catch some of them and rebuilt fences to keep them in. They were wonderful workers. My husband never got over how devoted they were.

AUDREY GERRED BECKLEY

The Salvation Army was unbelievable. I went to their tent by the Presbyterian church and the lady up there asked me what I needed. I told her I didn't need anything, but she asked me how many beds I had. She gave me new sheets.

I didn't feel that good about the Red Cross. I admit the first time I went in there I looked like something that had crawled out of the ground — because I had — but they made me feel like they were afraid to touch me.

I also felt like they weren't very respectful of where they were. Some of them smoked. Baptists don't allow smoking, especially in their church, and those people didn't respect that.

But there were people who just couldn't do enough for us. The people who lived across the street from us in Terrace Lake, where we stayed that summer, were Catholic. They had girls about my girls' ages. Every time they came back from church they'd bring us back something to eat. Guaranteed Foods was another place that was very helpful. We had just filled up our freezer full of food, and they came out the very next day. They took all our food they could salvage and stored it for us free of charge. Our dentist helped us by putting my fillings (which had blown out) back in and not charging us.

I'd ordered enough material from Sears to make summer outfits for all four girls. They took the cost of the material off my bill. I didn't ask them to, they just did it.

TREVA WOODLING

After we got out of the hospital we stayed at my aunt's house until our house was livable. Red Cross people came there and asked us a lot of questions about insurance. They decided we had too much insurance for them to help us.

We had people come to us in the hospital and give us money. They told us that they'd rather give it to us than the Red Cross.

PEGGY MCNAMARA

We went up to the Salvation Army tent next to the Presbyterian church. There was a pair of black patent-leather shoes that I really wanted. They were a half size too small, but so beautiful. I had no shoes left, and I wasn't wearing shoes when we ran to the basement so I needed something. These shoes were much too nice for everyday wear, and I don't think my mother would ever have bought them if we were shoe shopping. But I got them anyway.

NANCY EVANS

The church immediately came around offering help, and I felt guilty about taking anything. They wanted to give us money. I told them we didn't lose much, that they should be talking to people who needed everything.

We didn't have household insurance at that time, but our furniture was early Depression anyway, so I didn't worry that it was a little more pitted and scratched.

JEAN HENDERSHOT

Hank and Jim went around the next day to find out if they could help anyone. But by then the National Guard had things under control. Because they were in the area and trying to help, the Red Cross canteen people insisted they take box lunches. They said their houses weren't damaged, they shouldn't be eating food others might need, but they were reminded we all were without power and gas and no one was cooking that day.

AUSTIN SHUTE

You never knew who was going to reach out a hand to help. Guys I went to law school with raised some money for us. Another lawyer gave us a stove and refrigerator.

SHIRLEY GROSS

One thing we did was go over to our friends, who were in the hospital, with some other church members and go through their debris. They weren't in any shape to do it and it made us feel like we were maybe helping them recover a little. We were able to find a few of their valuables that way.

The Red Cross did an awful lot of good for us all, but I think people had a little different feeling about Red Cross than they did the Salvation Army. Many of the men had wartime experiences with Red Cross and, for one reason or another, came away with bad feelings. They were very businesslike, while the Salvation Army seemed to be based on Christian compassion, but both were there for us and helped a lot.

CLYDE OFNER JR.

The neighbors behind us hated dogs, including mine. They never liked my dog and my dog didn't like them. As it turned out, after the tornado the dog was gone. Our neighbor found him eight or nine blocks away and actually carried him, on foot, back to our house.

We were greatly served by the Salvation Army. They were right there when we needed them. I wore Salvation Army clothes for a year and so did my kids. Consequently, I've always given to them.

BILL MCCARTY

I was my own insurance agent, and I can tell you, I had the company's worst loss of the year.

The bank that our mortgage was with said it wasn't necessary to pay the principle while we were rebuilding, just to keep current with the interest for six months.

BOB AND JEAN MCCOY

Jean: I can't say anything but good about the Salvation Army and the Red Cross. The Salvation Army got us bedding and diapers right away, but the Red Cross found us a house. It was close by on Sycamore, and we were able to share it with the Northcrafts for the whole summer. It worked out great. We're still good friends.

Bob: Hallmark was real good to us. They sent someone out the next day and gave us one hundred dollars just so we'd have some cash. At a time of tragedy like that, it was a comfort to know I worked for such a generous company.

BILL AND MARY NORTHCRAFT

Mary: Bill was going to send the boys and me home on the train but we lost all our money and we couldn't afford it. Then Hallmark sent each of its employees who were hit one hundred dollars the next day. They were wonderful to us through the whole ordeal.

Bill: The Salvation Army were the first ones there with food and blankets. We also got some money from our church and from Red Cross. The Red Cross saved the day for us by getting that house we shared with the McCoys.

E.J. AND JEAN FROUNFELTER

Jean: I had all my pictures in a bread box. We didn't find the bread box, but when the Mennonites came they looked diligently and finally found some of the pictures buried in the debris. They put them in an envelope and mailed them to us.

I was a Girl Scout leader and E.J. was on the Girl Scout board committee in Independence. It wasn't more than a day before they brought a crib to the house where we were staying. Then we had a crib for both babies and Sally didn't have to sleep in the bathtub. Girl Scouts also sent us a box of clothes. I wore one of those dresses for years.

The Red Cross came by with their canteen serving coffee and sandwiches. They told us we should go to their office and apply for aid. We didn't know what would happen but they said, "You must come over," so we did. We were given one-hundred-dollars apiece allotment for clothes and shoes.

With the Salvation Army we didn't have to fill out forms. They just handed you things you'd need to rebuild your home. Slowly we were supplied with those things that are expensive to buy.

E.J.: I worked for Dun and Bradstreet at the time. They had a reporter for their newsletter interview me, and gave me a nice check from the office employees.

Jean: We had our dog with us, but our cat was missing. We called and we hunted, but didn't find him. We had been told that Wayside Waifs was sending trucks throughout the area, looking for lost pets. The ones they found they took back and cleaned them up. So we went to find old Tom there, and sure enough, he was. I took a little horse meat with me and as soon as he caught a whiff of that he started howling at me. We were sure glad to get our Tom back.

Wayside Waifs was so good. You don't think about all the number of pets that were lost, but you can imagine that there were a lot. Wayside Waifs rescued them. They put out food as bait and caught them as they came up out of basements and from under pockets of debris.

GLEN AND JEAN WILLIAMS

Jean: We heard from people we hadn't seen since high school. All of them sent money or offers to help.

A couple of Mennonite men just appeared. They helped us look for things. Then some people from Odessa, where we used to live, came up to help. I got so many checks in the mail from people I had to go to the bank every day to deposit them.

Certain things stick out in your mind. I remember a lady who lived just north, in Fairlaine, coming by with children's clothes. She said, "I went around to my neighbors and told them I didn't want used stuff. I wanted new things to give to the children of Ruskin."

Our glasses were lost that night, and we had to have them remade right away. There was a Lyon Optical store in Hickman Mills. They had made our glasses originally, and the store wasn't damaged, so we went back to have them remade. They made them free. We still get all our glasses there.

Over the years, I've heard bad things about the Red Cross, but I hate to knock them. They gave me certificates for shoes and wanted to give me two sets of sheets for each of us. Of course we had to get beds first. But they were very nice. I thought they wanted to give me more than I actually needed. I figured there were people who needed it worse than me.

Glen: The guys I worked with came out after a hard day at work and helped us move. I worked at A&P at a store in town. One of the guys used to set up a can by his cash register. He'd tell people to leave money because, "Glen needs money."

I was off seven weeks and they paid me full pay. And you know, I never remember even getting a medical bill.

JOE NESBIT

The Red Cross moved right in and started serving meals from the Burke kitchen. The kitchen part of the school wasn't hurt much, but we did have a problem with the roof over the all-purpose room where the meals were served. It didn't bother them or slow them down. I ate many meals there that summer.

Several of us principals worked at least five days a week salvaging school materials. We moved a lot of furniture around, and to different buildings, trying to get ready for the next school year. None of us got a vacation that summer, but no one complained. Just before school started, we all went down to the Lake of the Ozarks together for a long weekend.

LOUIS MANNEN

Since my school was in Independence I still had a school year to finish out. When I went back to work, later that week, teachers had brought boxes of clothing for me.

The Salvation Army set up a big tent by the Presbyterian church parking lot. You could go pick out anything you needed—shoes, dishes, clothes. They didn't question anyone's identity, and I know I saw people picking up things at that tent whose homes weren't damaged.

HELEN BOYLES

We had a charge account at Emery Bird Thayer. If you went to them and said, "Look, I've lost everything I bought from you," they'd say just forget the bill. I had recently bought a sewing machine from them and I was so proud of it. We found the head to it, and took it back, and they said to take my pick of new ones and they'd start our account over.

A fellow deacon told me I should go to Red Cross for help. My husband had a bad experience with Red Cross during the war, so I said, "Oh, they won't do anything." But this friend bet me a steak dinner that the Red Cross would help us, especially since we lost everything. I went to the office and filled out the forms and told them we lost everything. I never heard a thing. When the *Star* came out here to do the story on our house being rebuilt, he asked me if we had received any money from Red Cross. I told him my story. So the reporter called the Red Cross office to check it out. Before I knew it, I got a call from Red Cross complaining to me that I had complained. But I ended up getting my money, only because of the reporter, and I had to buy my friend a steak dinner.

SIDNEY BATES

My Boy Scout troop worked that summer with the Red Cross breaking into lockers from the junior high and high school. We emptied them and sorted the stuff out to be distributed at Westridge school. We found a lot of gym shoes and water pistols.

CHARLES GRAY

There's a plaque in an elevator at city hall from the people of Ruskin, thanking the people of Kansas City.

JOE KRAMER

Right after the tornado there was a lot of talk about it being God's reminder to us of his presence among us. I thought, good Lord, unless you believe in an apocalyptic God, that statement was very out of place considering the grieving circumstances. A random occurrence of nature I don't think is an act of God. Although by law I guess that's what it's considered. But to me all of the wonderful, decent, humanitarian things that people did for one another, that to me was the evidence of the presence of God.

Ruskin Shopping Center seen from behind

Mennonites in Hickman Mills

Sea of debris

Unclaimed cars at Ruskin Shopping Center

A SYMBOL OF HOPE

VIII

No church bells rang at the Presbyterian church that Sunday morning, May 26. The congregation came anyway. They came to be together where they felt safe, where many of them sought shelter that past Monday night. It was too much to comprehend that only last Sunday the main topic of conversation had been the first anniversary of the church's dedication: dedicated on May 20, 1956, destroyed May 20th 1957. Now they huddled together in prayer, trying not to think of the horror and death that had littered the church grounds. The best way to dim those images was to rebuild.

The day before in the parking lot of the shopping center, a mass meeting sponsored by the Ruskin Homes Association had done much to answer questions and calm fears about insurance, disaster aid and rebuilding. The cost of the storm totaled $75 million. Governor Blair's request for $25 million in disaster aid was already under President Eisenhower's consideration, and people were anxious to know what it would cover. Austin Shute, as president of the Homes Association, introduced representatives from the Red Cross, Salvation Army, Civil Defense, FHA, Veterans Administration, Small Business Administration, American Legion, and K.C. Mortgage Company, as well as those who could help answer questions about taxes and the school arrangements. It was emphasized that Praver and Sons Reconstruction Company planned to set up a temporary office in Sycamore Park, but that home owners were under no obligation to use Praver again. To start the meeting, H. Roe Bartle spoke to the crowd. Father Joseph Ruysser from St. Catherine's Catholic Church gave the closing prayer. The community wasted no time bouncing back.

A carpenter's strike in early June delayed projected plans for many. Already, 111 families had signed up with the Pravers to start construction. Some carpenters and contractors came to an "understanding" to continue work in the stricken area, but for the most part, construction halted. During the strike, one union official stated, "The carpenter's union is deeply sympathetic to the needs of the tornado victims. There are forty families of our own members among the sufferers." It was a public-relations nightmare, and a settlement was soon reached. In spite of setbacks, the first family moved into their reconstructed home within the month. Howard (Skeeter) Boyles, his wife Helen, and their daughter Libby, proudly posed for a picture in front of their house with Mayor Bartle and mortgage officials. Stanley Praver handed the keys to Mr. Boyles. A spokesman for Praver Reconstruction Company stated later that week that they were able to raise and sheath in six houses a day. Already Veteran Administration inspectors had inspected 420 houses. Demolition was scheduled for the remaining walls of Ruskin Center and reconstruction would begin soon. Merchants would be in business again in time for the Christmas season. This was the beginning. People were ready to reclaim their neighborhoods.

But nature wasn't quite ready to let go. The storms were frequent and fierce that summer, and everyone in the area felt more vulnerable than ever. Nightmares were very close to the surface. As residents looked out at turbulent skies, at lots still uncleared and overgrown with tenacious clumps of grass, at old friends constructing new lives, neighborhood never meant so much.

So many were still in hospitals, so much pain lingered. Edith Dixon, the grandmother who broke Steve Johnston's fall — and thereby her leg — remained in the hospital for three months. Two years and four operations later, she was healed. Virginia Bramble, thrown from the car that hit the water tower, became the last casualty to leave the hospital. By the end of September, she was home but confined to bed. Although her head injuries were severe, she eventually recovered.

There were good times too. The Optimist Club set up a rock-and-roll canteen on the football field of the high school. By the second night after the tornado this tent was full of Ruskin students dancing and playing Ping-Pong. Throughout the summer there was an afternoon session for junior high students, and the high school kids took over in the evenings. With the silhouette of the gymnasium arches in the background, teenagers began to heal to the sounds of Chuck Berry and Elvis.

In this spring of storms, many throughout the country experienced similar situations, connecting our stories to a larger story. *Life* magazine did a feature article on the turbulent weather and spotlighted southern Jackson County. *Time* magazine, *Saturday Review* and *American Mercury* all reported on our tornado. On Memorial Day, William Peck and his family appeared on Art Linkletter's

Houseparty television show. Chosen as a typical Ruskin family, they told of their race to the Presbyterian church basement. Mr. Peck had looked back just in time to see the shopping center destroyed, and drew his impression of that sight for the studio audience.

My parents seriously considered not moving back. We spent much of the summer driving around other suburban developments in the Kansas City area looking for something to replace what we had lost. Our neighbors moved back in throughout the summer, and right before school started, we did too. David and I got flashlights to keep close by our beds, just in case, and we settled in. "Before the tornado" became a phrase we used over and over again, our own little crinkle of time. That first evening, when my parents visited over the fence with the McNamaras while all of us kids played tag, they knew they had chosen the right neighborhood. It wasn't lost after all.

JIM AND AGGIE TURNBAUGH
Jim: We worked day and night getting *Twilight Twister* ready to print. We wanted to tell the story while it was fresh and to show how courageous people where. We saw an awful lot of inner strength. The causalities of this thing dug themselves out and rebuilt and always thought someone else needed more help than they did. The book was available within two weeks and we couldn't print enough to keep up with the demand.
Aggie: A lot of businesses put ads in our paper saying they'd be back. They just didn't know how badly hurt they were. They were trying to be brave. About half of them were out of business without knowing it; the degree of devastation hadn't caught up with them yet. The other half were hurt horribly and would have a tough time bouncing back. It was months before they could get buildings up and stocked.

STANLEY JEPPESEN
My wife had a nervous breakdown over the tornado. She kept everything bottled up, and about a year later she had a really hard time. I had nightmares for a long time, along with the constant pain. For almost fifteen years my leg was basically useless. I had nine operations on it over that time. I went over a year one time without work because no one will hire you with a broken leg. The doctor took my hip off twice. Once I told him to just cut the damn thing off, I was sick of messing with it, but he told me I'd have to find

another doctor if that was my plan. I could take my leg halfway between the knee and the ankle and just bend it. I had ridden horses all my life, and used to do rodeos, but that was over. It was a hard thing to adjust to.

Sheryl had nightmares too, and was scared to death of storms, especially that summer. It didn't take much to set her off and that was a bad summer for storms. We were always running for shelter. But half of her problem was the adults.

SHERYL JEPPESEN MCKINNEY

Dad was in the hospital the longest, but I was there for eight or nine days. After I got home, I had to stay in a baby crib for a long time because I couldn't walk.

My grandfather was banged up pretty badly and I knew he wouldn't let the doctors mess with him. But I believe it took him more than a few days to get back to normal. It wasn't just shock. He really wasn't himself. He was disoriented.

Even though Mom wasn't hurt as badly physically, she had a very tough time emotionally. We had just been in this big car wreck the year before, and she had almost died that time. Now this tornado. The next year we moved to Hickman Mills, into a house that had been damaged, and the neighbors always reacted to storms with a lot of fear. None of this helped.

The tornado stayed with us kids in a different way. There was a vacant lot next to our house and we played there all the time. For years we'd dig up strange things. We always thought it was normal to dig in a yard and find weird things.

ELINOR STEINBRUECK

Two weeks later I took the girls to some relatives in Hutchinson, Kansas. I rode with some people who were storm trackers. On the way down there, the driver could tell there was a bad storm brewing because of the air turbulence. He could tell we were driving right into it, but didn't say anything then. When we got to Hutchinson he took us to his house because he knew our relatives didn't have a basement, and we went to his basement immediately. A funnel cloud went right over us there.

It took quite awhile for our house to be rebuilt, but we liked going over there to see other neighbors checking on their property. I remember on the Fourth of July we went over and sat on the front step and watched fireworks. We had a clear view because all the trees were gone.

LOREN GAYDUSEK
Our house was picked up and set back down. The ceiling in the kitchen was raised up about one inch. The insurance company wanted to do a lot more work on our house, but I just wanted to settle. I didn't feel like we had time to spare. We moved back in the 23rd of August, and my wife had twin boys in September.

MARIALICE ETEM
Since my husband was the insurance man for so many of our Hickman Mills and Ruskin friends, I didn't see much of him that summer. He never worked so hard. Not everyone was lucky enough to have such a devoted insurance company. There was one house on our block where the people couldn't get a settlement with their insurance company. So they put up a huge sign, it was eight feet long and four feet high, that said, "We have insurance with..."— they named the company — "and they haven't settled yet." The company was out there the next day.

WILLIS AND MAXINE WATKINS
Willis: We were at the point where we had a two-bedroom house and three kids. We were wondering how in the world we could add another bedroom to this house and still meet FHA requirements. There just wasn't any good way to do it. Well, the tornado solved that problem for us.
Maxine: You lost things that you didn't even think of for a while. That next fall when the kids went back to school they needed their birth certificates. Well, we had kept them in a cigar box on a closet shelf and they were gone. We hadn't even thought of them until then.

WALT BODINE
We talked to so many people during that first twenty-four hours that the station decided to put together a radio special on the tornado. We did it in three parts and included interviews with policemen and doctors as well as residents. So much happened so quickly that we felt the city needed an overview of events that

night. We called it *Diary of a Disaster,* and it was broadcast within the week. It was a very effective radio documentary.

Everyone paid very close attention to our weather reports that summer, but after a while we got complaints about all the coverage. The problem is, right after a tornado the public forgives us if we post a warning and nothing happens. Two years after a big storm they'll still go to the basement, but they're irritated if nothing happens. I always thought that was strange.

REV. LOREN GOINGS

The Baptist church was undamaged, and of course it became a hub of activity because the Red Cross was stationed there. But that next Sunday was very hard on people. I don't remember what sermons I had prepared, but after the tornado came I preached two sermons about God loving us. I thought that was important. We needed to be reminded.

Our church was deeply in debt with our new building, and my thought was, we're in trouble now. One couple had lost everything, including their offertory envelopes. The next Sunday they were there with an old battered-up envelope with their money in it. Financially, we didn't suffer a bit. It was remarkable.

MARTA SCHUMACHER

That summer while our house was being rebuilt we lived in a twenty-seven foot trailer parked on our lot. Six adults. After a couple of weeks we were all out of the hospital so we were all there for quite a while. Later on, my aunt and uncle and brother slept in the basement, and Mom, my sister and I slept in the trailer. But we had our meals at the little table in the trailer.

PETE KOTSIFAKIS

Every evening we'd come out to the lot and our neighbors, the Schumachers, would be raking their yard of debris. They'd say, "Might as well use this wood for a fire and roast hot dogs and marshmallows and invite the neighbors." Every night we had something to do. The Schumachers entertained us.

We spent a lot of time raking our yard too. But even with all the rubble we hauled out of there, we didn't get anywhere near all of it. We have a garden out back, and for years we dug up pieces of things. We found a lot of plumbing.

A guy came in with a truck and said, "I'll help you clean up your place if you let me take all the scrap metal." I said sure, so he just took the scrap metal and left. There were a lot of those kind of people.

I'm an electrical engineer, and it just seemed to me that it would be possible to build some kind of a tornado detector. A bunch of us from Bendix decided to build a device. The Spherics, we called it. The government was interested and experimented with it, but they said there were so many types of tornadoes that it wouldn't work for all of them.

Will Witty was the main designer, and I built it to his specifications. I built the first model. In fact, I've still got it. Once I had it in a bedroom with antenna all around and another one at our next door neighbors, the Hembrees.

One day I heard the thing screaming and not a cloud in the sky, and I said, "That darn thing, its not any good." So I went over to Hembrees and tried to shut the thing off and it didn't want to shut off. Finally I got it off and came back home. My family told me that it had just come over the radio: Emporia, Kansas was under a tornado warning. That's about where our tornado had started.

ANNA LEE HEMBREE

I didn't come back for a couple of days because Judy was so sick. We just stayed in Raytown with our family. But when I did try to go in, without a purse or I.D., the National Guard wouldn't let me in. My husband was already in the area at our house, so he didn't know I couldn't get in. Luckily a friend of ours took me to get an identification card and vouched for who I was.

After that we tried to go over whenever we could. Everyone had to work their jobs, but on weekends and evenings we'd all be out here doing what we could and just being close to each other.

CLYDE RENKEN

We had just bought a mahogany dining room set. We never saw one piece of it again except one drawer sitting in the backyard with tablecloths in it.

Jackson County said to throw all the debris from your house out along the road. They were going to come pick it up. Instead, they came with a road grader and pushed it all back up on our property. They had told us if it was off our property they'd pick it up. Well, they picked it up all right, they pushed it right back on our property.

When people started moving things in, the looters showed up again. To keep anybody from stealing our things, we moved back out as soon as we had a bath and cooking facilities. But I'd just lay there at night with a shotgun laying right along the side of the bed and thought, First head that shows up at that window is gone.

Then it was income-tax time. I went down to Internal Revenue and asked how do you figure this loss on the place. They said to have a real estate broker tell you what the house was worth at noon the day before the tornado, then tell you how much it was worth the day after. Subtract that figure, and anything not covered by insurance, take it off. So that's what I went by.

What happens? Next year they call me down. They said, "Well, we know that's the law, but we don't go by that. You can only take off what you can prove that you paid in." I said, "How can I get the papers to prove that when those papers flew to Iowa somewhere?" So they got me to pay $500 after losing everything.

DONNA BRAMBLE WILLIAMS

The nurses were wonderful. I got the best care that could be given. It was difficult to keep me comfortable. There was no air-conditioning, and my wounds would stick to the sheets, but they did everything possible to help me and make me feel cared for. Everyone wanted to help. One of the doctors had a son whose birthday was the same as mine, June 9, so he brought me in a fourth of his son's birthday cake. There was a photographer visiting the ward, and he wanted to take my picture. I was so self-conscious of my missing front teeth, I asked him not to. He promised to come back when I had healed and got false teeth and take a real portrait of me. He did too. Then there was a man who came in every day to brush my hair. My scalp was full of mud and debris, and it took a long time to get everything out because it hurt so badly, but he was very patient and kind.

THELMA KIRKMAN

Lou Davis was our original salesman and closed the deal on our house. Part of what sold us on the house was his describing how cool this spot was, and how, because it was high ground, a breeze would blow through our house. When we saw him after the tornado, we told him he had been right, but we no longer appreciated that selling point.

MIKE ANGOTTI

We were able to take our storage shed that had been in the back of the shopping center and straighten it out enough to use it. We moved it out in front of the store and reopened with what merchandise we saved. A lot of the housewares we donated to the Salvation Army tent there in the parking lot. People needed their hardware store as they repaired and rebuilt, so we were happy to reopen as soon as we could.

JEANNE JOHNSTON GORMAN

That summer was pure hell. I'd lost my husband, and my boys were still recuperating. Our house was livable, but being out there with the constant reminder every time I looked out the window, was very hard. When you go through a traumatic time like that, it's funny what kind of things stick in your mind. One of the things that was most upsetting to me was grocery shopping. The A&P was gone and the Crest Market in Hickman Mills was closed while it was being rebuilt. There weren't any other grocery stores out there. It was awful. I had to go all the way to Raytown to get groceries.

JEAN HAYES

When we first moved to Ruskin, we planted a silver maple in our front yard. The tornado broke it off and split the trunk. It never grew back like a normal tree, but became our silver-maple bush.

Like everyone else, I went out and unloaded what was left in cabinets and packed things away. But I didn't want to be out there much.

BETTY HAMBEL

You do what you have to do and go to pieces later. That summer was so hard on all of us. We had one tornado sighting after another. We were able to move back in pretty quickly, so there we were with vacant lots still all over, so it was constantly with us. We hadn't built our storm cellar. The man next door had a station-wagon, and we were in that car constantly, running. It was sheer panic.

HERB GREEN

After they started building all the houses back, the police caught this guy over on the next street in a truck full of doors. Some contractor had a deal to build ten houses back. They put the doors in one day, and that night this guy came in and lifted them all.

He was caught and the doors were taken back. For about two days you'd see guys running up and down the street with doors, trying to figure out which one was theirs, because they weren't interchangeable.

ART PETERSON

It was strange that summer. We'd get up in the morning and look toward the destruction and see no homes on the block behind us. It was sort of spooky.

Our kids were afraid. They didn't want to come home from their grandparents'. So we borrowed a dump truck and hauled a whole load of stuff away. We tacked up some plastic over our windows until we could get them replaced. Of course, every little bit of wind movement would make a noise. It was hard to sleep for a while.

A lot of our neighbors had our house key and knew to come in— even if we weren't home— if there were storms. We had the only basement on this end of the block, so when the weather got bad we started expecting visits from the neighbors. There were twenty-five in our basement the night of the tornado. The next week we had another warning, and there were a lot more than twenty-five here.

We wanted a double garage when we bought our Ruskin house, but the Praver plans had no double garages. We lived on a corner lot and had plenty of room, so after the tornado we figured this was our chance to customize our house. Not only did we get our double garage, but we built a screened in patio too.

MERYL OSTERGARD

I got involved in the cleanup and didn't go back to work for thirty days. One of the first things I did was help with the construction of the dance tent on the football field. We had it ready for the kids almost immediately. Truman Corners was just barely opened, and the north corner of it was badly damaged. Eighty percent of the Western Auto stock was gone. I offered to store what was left in my garage and basement. There was a tremendous amount of work to do at Ruskin Center. I worked in both the shoe store and the toy store, trying to go through things. Both stores were able to salvage some things, but not much. Everyone moved back though.

MARJORIE LANGFORD

While I was in the hospital, I prepared myself mentally for going home. My husband had described our house and the school, so I was ready to face that. The thing that upset me the most were the trees. I just wasn't prepared to see them gone.

Center High School offered their gym for Ruskin's graduation. Center had a policy of never walking down the center aisle of their gym. It was a tradition of school pride, like at Ruskin never stepping on the inlay eagle in the front hall. But Ruskin graduates had practiced walking down the middle at home so Center allowed them to do it that way.

It was a heartbreaking ceremony. There were seventy-four graduates and most of them had been affected by the tornado. One of them was the son of the school janitor who had been killed. The student body president's family had lost everything, including his cap and gown.

One of the songs that the choir had prepared for that night was, "You'll Never Walk Alone," which starts out, "When you walk through a storm hold your head up high." Before the tornado, I had heard them practicing, and they did a fabulous job. I told the choir director how effective it was, and he said, "Marge, I'm going to let you set up the crying towel stand." They went ahead and sang it at graduation, and believe me, we needed more than towels.

That next fall the high school was at Burke, and they farmed the grade school kids out to the other grade schools. There were all kinds of makeshift arrangements at first. The elective classes were the ones we moved around the most. Burke's kindergarten room became the band room and the shop classes were in the administration building. That meant those students had to be bussed to that building and to the quickly reconstructed gym for classes there.

RUSS MILLIN

Sheriff Owsley called me one day and said that Senator Stuart Symington was coming to assess the damage and to help us make application for disaster-relief funds. He said he thought that because I was president of the Hickman Mills Chamber of Commerce and lived in Ruskin I should meet him and give him a tour of the area. These were in the early days of my career as a defense attorney and I was just getting my political feet wet, so it sounded like a good idea to me.

After the initial meeting, we met downtown at the federal court house in Symington's office with the state auditor and lawyers for the construction company the school superintendent, Carl Wagner, had already hired. We had to open the bid for construction to everyone, so it was a little sticky, but Symington did a marvelous job of getting things ironed out. The money started flowing. Ultimately we received one million dollars to rebuild the schools.

After things had settled down and we knew we were going to have to build another new grade school, I got a call from a fellow school board member. This man was a Republican and I'm a Democrat. He said, "Why don't we name our new school after Symington." So I called Washington and told the senator he had our bipartisan support for naming the school after him. He was pleased.

Here's a little known anecdote. There were five young attorneys and their families living in the Ruskin Heights or Hickman Mills area at the time. That storm took a line through the communities from southwest to northeast that caught the home of every lawyer.

BLAINE STECK

The high school was built back with a grant from the government. The old brick junior high building was torn down and the new high school extended up into that area. The building was built back so a third floor could be added. It was most unfortunate that the building was destroyed, but the community and district were better off. They got so much more back. The gymnasium was built pretty much like it was before. The arches were replaced because no engineering firm would approve their safety. They might have been safe but no one wanted to take a chance on them. So they had the present beams shipped in from Oregon.

We spent the summer trying to get ready for the fall. You couldn't ask for better cooperation and support from the staff. I'm not aware of anyone not coming back because of the changed facilities. I think most of them came back wanting to help, and realized, hey, this isn't ideal but we'll make it work. You can do lots of things if you have to. The teachers and students accepted that. It's one of the things that molded the community together. I'd have to say I didn't hear too much complaining.

JOE NESBIT

One of the things the tornado did to the community that I remember so well was that we, the board of education and the administration, had a lot of pressure to build shelters in the school buildings. We decided we couldn't do that because we hardly had enough room for students. So there was a kind of compromise that satisfied the parents, I guess, and helped us too. Whenever there was a tornado alert issued on television or radio we called the bus company and they took the children home. The awful thought was what if another one hit with the children in the schools? What if the tornado had been a night later and the high school graduation was going on? The other thing that it did to the school system was put the high school in Burke for 1957-58. We had to find a place for the junior high, so we divided up the all-purpose rooms in Johnson and Westridge and Truman and put those seventh and eighth graders in the elementary schools for the next year.

Symington and his staff here in Kansas City were quite helpful in getting the wheels moving and cutting through red tape. When they decided to rebuild Ruskin, they set up a plan with the architect where they just said that a room was to be so wide and so long, and the hall was to be so long, and we had all kinds of red tape. Normally, a contractor was to get a bond to insure he'd finish the building. In order for a bonding company to allow a bond, they want to see the complete set of architectural plans for the building and approve them. Well, we were just coming up out of the ground, building as we could. Senator Symington's staff stepped in, and I don't know what strings he pulled, but he said, "Now look, these people have really got a problem. You go ahead and bond the builder and let them get underway." There was disaster aid in which the government would allow you to construct as many square feet of space as you lost. I remember going to Jefferson City with the superintendent and sitting down with the officials. Again, they wanted to see complete plans, which normally we would want them to see, but in our case we wanted to get the building built back in time for classes in the fall. Symington, in particular, put his pressure on the politicians to get these officials to go ahead. That's the reason for Symington Elementary School.

TREVA WOODLING

Harry fought his way out of the hospital to go to Denise's funeral. I was in traction, so my going was out of the question. He shouldn't have gone either. He was running a fever and still badly injured. But to him it was very important to be there.

While I was in the hospital, I didn't look at any of the papers or the news on television. I didn't want to see anything about the tornado. By the time I got home, most of the debris was cleaned up in the area and our house was fixed. But the sightseers weren't gone completely. Harry had our wrecked car pulled up in the driveway waiting for the insurance settlement. People actually knocked on our door and asked what happened to us. We had to ask the same question sometimes. Within the year Dean developed aplastic anemia and wasn't expected to live. He could just fall and hemorrhage internally, so we had to always watch him. He couldn't ride a tricycle or play like other kids, and you just hated to keep him from living a normal life. No one ever said the tornado caused this, but the fact that he was so badly bruised made us wonder. He lived for another seven years.

Diane recovered completely, but she did have to go back to the hospital to have a piece of wood removed from her back. The doctors wouldn't let me go into the operating room with her and she was so scared. She just cried and cried. I was really mad. What would it have hurt to put a gown on me and let me hold her hand?

Diane and I got out of the hospital in about four weeks. Dean had been out awhile and was staying with relatives. We were all driving home together for the first time, Diane and Dean in the backseat. Harry and I had decided we'd wait until we got home and then tell the kids about Denise. Diane had never asked about her because we all ended up in different hospitals. So she just thought Denise was somewhere else. Preparing myself to tell her was the hardest thing that ever was. We were almost home and all of a sudden Diane said, "Well, Mother, where's Denise?" and I wanted to wait until we got home to tell her. But I went ahead and looked back at her. She was just as white as a sheet, and I said, "Honey, she died in the tornado." That was the most difficult thing I've ever had to tell her. I wanted to hold her while I explained, but I couldn't with her in the backseat. I never thought I'd have any more problems after the tornado because I could walk and everything. So I got pregnant soon, not dreaming there was any reason not to. I thought if we had another baby it would take Harry's mind off Denise. He was really getting bitter toward God because we'd lost Denise. But our troubles were just beginning. When our baby was born he started turning blue. They worked frantically to keep him alive, but he only lived a few hours.

A few months after I got pregnant, I started having troubles.

The more I'd use my arms, the more pain I'd have right between my shoulder blades. I also got numbness in both legs. The doctor thought it was the pressure from the baby, but when it didn't go away after the baby was born, he figured it was something else. What we discovered is that wood doesn't show up on X-rays. I had three major operations on my spine as a result of a piece of wood that blew in where all the roofing nails were. The first was right after the baby was born. There were all kinds of doctors sitting in on the operation. They cut in up by my neck and found a splinter of wood with a piece of the red blouse I was wearing the day of the tornado still wrapped around it. It was between two vertebrae and had scar tissue around it. I guess those doctors about fell through the floor.

Two years later I started having trouble walking. That's when I had the second operation. This time they discovered that scar tissue from the first operation had surrounded the spinal cord and was choking it. While the surgeon was fixing that, he noticed another spot of something further down on my spine, but he didn't do anything about it because he was afraid he'd leave me paralyzed.

Two years after that, all of a sudden my legs gave away one day. I ended up at Mayo's. The doctor up there told me I would die if I didn't have an operation, and there was only a fifty-fifty chance I'd make it through surgery, and if I did I'd be paralyzed. When he removed the spot that the first doctor had seen, they discovered it had grown to the size of a marble inside my spinal cord and had severed it almost in two. The pathologist seemed to think it was fragments of paint and debris from the tornado that scar tissue formed around. This was five years after the tornado and I've been paralyzed ever since.

When I was in the hospital after the tornado I was in traction and in so much pain. I couldn't stand to have anyone touch me, it hurt so much. I just laid there and prayed the Twenty-third Psalm. And I'd say to God, well, if Jesus could stand dying on the cross then surely I can stand this. That's how I got through it. Each day I'd feel a little bit stronger.

AUDREY BECKLEY GERRED

That Fourth of July was awful. My girls had a hard time with loud noises for a long time. Every time I turned around that Independence Day I had four girls hanging on to my shirttails.

Before the tornado we had made quite a few improvements on

our house and we put more down to begin with than was required. All that meant we were underinsured and couldn't get enough reimbursement from our insurance company to replace everything. We decided the best thing was to not move back. But we didn't go far. We just moved a little to the east into Ruskin Hills. Now I'm back on my old block living in the house with the basement we went to that night.

A tragedy like the tornado affects people differently. I know some families who didn't pull together and it split them apart. I felt it drew us closer.

HELEN BOYLES

We didn't plan to be the first family back in. It just worked out that way. But seeing our house go up so fast must have been a symbol of hope for everyone driving by. Praver was smart. He built this house and showed everyone: "I'll get you back in here quickly." Now, I'm sure others didn't get their houses built as quickly as we did. But his idea was to show the community his commitment to rebuilding.

This is a funny thing to remember, but the only time I cried was over a philodendron. I had a flower stand with this house plant in it that just seemed to be in the way. Someone was always knocking it over and I'd have to clean up the mess. When we were going through stuff I thought of that plant and that's what made me cry. I didn't even like the dang thing.

DEAN AND NANCY EVANS

Dean: Before Nancy came home I had a big scare. You can't imagine how still it is with no people moving around, no cars, no lights. One night I was working in the house, cleaning up, and I heard numerous footsteps coming up the street. They came right up the driveway. I got a ball bat ready to defend myself. There was a knock and I positioned myself to start swinging against this mob. I opened the door and there stood my preacher, Harry Dale Collier, and about ten guys with him asking if I needed any help. I was so embarrassed I turned them down.

Praver contracted to have debris taken to Sycamore Park, which was right down the street from us. Great big earth movers excavated a hole that was so large you could drive a truck down into it. They piled the dirt into an enormous hill. Then the dump trucks backed up and dumped into it. When the hole was filled they put the dirt back over it and the park was a little higher than it was before. Everything went in there. From our house they hauled off the roofing that they replaced, and that debris from the back wall, and a garage door that came from somewhere else, even chain-link fencing.

It was pretty expensive getting all that cleaned out. Here's this $11,400 house we had and we spent almost $7,000 fixing it back up. I think it was cheaper to build the neighbor's house across the street because it was swept clean. They didn't have to clean away all the torn down stuff.

Nancy: Rebuilding was an experience in itself. I'm sure I was back by about eight to ten days. By then you could hear bulldozers all day long.

Our house was not severely damaged, and I'm sure every carpenter in Kansas City was already hired. The old guy who came to do our work would never have been working if everyone in town hadn't been employed. He couldn't see, and he could hardly get up and down. I mean he was elderly. Our daughter, Cynthia, would find things he'd drop on the floor, like screws, and give them back to him because the guy couldn't see. I don't know how he ever got our house put back together.

Actually, we ended up with a better house. We always joked that we bought a new house and when we finished it was newer. After the tornado we had better windows, a better garage door, better landscaping.

It seems to me we got the Presbyterian church built back pretty quickly. I know people came back there to church all summer. We all still regarded the area as home, even if most people were living elsewhere for a while. And we needed our church and each other. Even though the building was gone we weren't giving up on it.

The horror was never far from our thoughts though. Those old pasteboard tables out of Fellowship Hall in the church had been used as stretchers and they were stained with blood. We had to work around that until we could replace them.

Dean: Because I was a reporter, I remember hearing a lot of talk about tornado detection. The civil authorities tried all kinds of things. One of the atmospheric reactions associated with tornadoes is the barometric pressure goes up minutes before a tornado occurs. So they put barrels around town with a valve on them that would react to this pressure jump. They were keyed into an alarm system in a central office somewhere. The problem was, to work they needed a vast network of these and a lot of barrels and a lot of wire. Over the years the improvements in radar technology made all other methods obsolete.

LOUIS MANNEN

We had our house up for sale at the time of the tornado. Since I worked in Independence, I wanted to move closer. So we didn't do anything about rebuilding the house. We just sold the lot back to Praver.

JOE KRAMER

The Pravers came and gouged out huge holes in Sycamore Park. Bulldozers took debris away and dumped it in this pit and set it on fire. There was a pall of smoke for days and days. One of the most remarkable things was how quickly all the wreckage was swept up and dumped into this fire pit. It seemed like a well-conceived and skillfully executed plan to get the place cleaned up so people could resume some semblance of normal living.

We also seemed to get our schools up and running pretty smoothly. We had a young school superintendent, Dr. Carl Wagner. Thanks to Senator Symington and other law- makers we were getting a lot of disaster-relief funding, much of it was going to the schools. Ruskin High School was a fairly new school at the time, but pretty badly wrecked. Dr. Wagner asked whatever federal authorities he would have asked, whether it was necessary to reconstruct Ruskin as it was, or could the money be spent to produce a more efficient facility. They said, "Hey, it's your money. Spend it the way you feel it should be spent, as long as it meets the purpose that it formally served." He had it redesigned for more efficiency, more usable space for educational purposes. He used the federal aid proceeds from that disaster to very beneficial effect.

There was so much information coming in so fast, it was hard to keep the public up to date. We were still giving information on the injured and their condition, looking for people and reporting on the rebuilding plans all at once. I had a weekly television show on Sunday afternoon called *This Week In Kansas City* , on KCMO, and that next Sunday we devoted an entire hour to the tornado.

The tornado made a big difference in how we reported weather.

The years I was news director at KCMO we were very conscious of informing the public of bad weather. Frankly, we overreacted. We were coming from nothing in the way of reporting tornado coverage. We had no concept of what to do and then, when we figured out what we should have done, we started doing it every time a little black cloud squeezed out a raindrop. I can remember spending literally hours of time on the air, sometimes in front of television cameras, as we rather obsessively reported everything we knew and could find out about tornado sightings, tornado touchdowns, tornado damage.

JEAN HENDERSHOT

We were a very small library and we didn't want to lose any books. We'd just been there in the shopping center a little over a year. People came out from Jackson County Library headquarters and took all the books in. For three weeks the lady I worked with and I went every day and cleaned up all the books. When we'd go home we'd be so dirty. It's possible we still might have a few of those books on our shelves. You wouldn't have believed we could clean them up to use again, but we did.

We borrowed a Kansas City public service bus and put it in the parking lot of the shopping center. It was terribly, terribly hot, but that library was used. People had nothing else to do and boy, did they ever read that summer. It was an unforgettable summer. People were very skittish. Every time there was a storm, and there were plenty of them that year, everyone would think tornado. But the thing I had the hardest time with was the trees. They were all just completely denuded, nothing but bare branches, all the limbs blown off. They looked so grotesque standing there. It took a couple summers for them to start looking like trees again, but they did. For a while it was such a reminder just to look at the trees and think what had happened to them.

AUSTIN SHUTE

I had all the work I could handle trying to get things settled. Russ (Millin) was busy getting the schools rebuilt, and he did a great job. But there were a lot of things we had to do, or the community would never have been rebuilt. That was the purpose of the mass meeting the Saturday after the tornado. We on the Homes Association board knew that people had questions and problems, and it was the only way to address everyone at once.

The Ruskin Homes Association voted to let Praver use the park to put debris in. There were some complaints about that, particularly the smoke, but I think most people realized all that rubble had to go somewhere before the Pravers and other contractors could rebuild. There are always a few though. I was even accused of being paid off by the Pravers, I'm not sure why to this day. People could have whomever they wanted build their house back.

Then we had some trouble with the FHA inspectors. They didn't want to inspect the rebuilt homes to make sure they were rebuilt properly. The builders could have put up anything they wanted and the home owners would be stuck with it. We made a few calls and got that one straightened out.

We had to handle all kinds of things, some easier than others. We had a pretty active train line right there between Burke school and the shopping center, and those trains sounded just like a tornado. People coming up to me there at my trailer in front of the high school mentioned how frightened they were of that sound. So we called Kansas City Southern and explained the situation. From then on the engineers blew the whistle as they approached that intersection.

DELORES SCHUENEMEYER

We had a lot of broken windows and screens. Even though we could live there we had no way of securing the house. It seemed to take forever for us to get an insurance settlement because it was such minor damage compared to other people. All that time I was afraid of looting. In fact, between the looting and the storms, I was nervous the whole summer. We finally ended up settling for a lot less than we expected. But we were grateful to have a home.

A friend offered to take my kids for a few days so we could clean up without worrying about them stepping on something. When they came back our five year old cried and said, "I thought it would look better."

SHIRLEY GROSS

You were almost better off losing everything because then there was no question of insurance paying for new things. But in our case the insurance company wanted to refinish furniture and rebuild our car rather than replace it. That car was never quite right again. I was doing income taxes at that time and it was a mess getting that all straightened out. People from the tornado would come to me with lists of things that had been lost, and I'd have to say, "Do you have any way of proving it?" You'd just have to trust people were honest. But some weren't. Years later, when I was selling real estate in Ruskin I was showing a house and the owner said to me that every time she walked down the hallway she worried about the attic fan falling on her head. I asked her why, and she said, "Because we didn't have one before the tornado and I told the insurance company we did."

CLYDE OFNER JR.

The insurance company we had on our mortgage went under because of the high number of homes they had in that area. We wound up having to sue them to get any money. When we finally did settle they didn't reimburse us for the land because it, in fact, was still there. So then we had to sell that piece of land. Whoever bought the land had to put a new house up.

I did take a little bit of the Ruskin house with us when we moved. I was able to salvage some of the water pipes and I made a jungle gym swing set for my boys out of them.

E.J. AND JEAN FROUNFELTER

Jean: It took wrecking balls forever to get Ruskin Junior High knocked down the rest of the way. I was sitting in the car while E.J. was talking to some insurance people in a trailer out front of the school. While I sat there the big wrecking balls had to strike it over and over again to get any part of it to budge. It was amazing to see how strong that building actually was when the tornado took a large part of it with no trouble at all. But to get it down completely was a real struggle.

E.J.: Another of the friends that loaned us their house for a couple weeks discovered later their house was damaged more than they thought. The force of the wind popped nails. It was strange. Some of the houses on the edge of the path had obvious damage right away inside, with buckled walls and so forth. But weeks and even months later some of the houses showed up where walls had definite damage from suction. It actually made the drywall move. So those covered nail heads started sticking out. Some people already had insurance settlements, and then they had to go back and resettle.

Jean: Our insurance covered the rebuilding of the house, and we had some contents insurance. It wasn't enough, but we had it. We tried our best to budget what we bought to fit the settlement.

We had a little fun redecorating. All those houses were painted just alike and now we could customize and paint any color we wanted. So I said, "Let's do a black living room wall, just for the hell of it." Of course the painters about had a fit. But I said, "Oh, you can do it." I had pink and gold accents and it was a lovely room.

GLEN AND JEAN WILLIAMS

Jean: Glen and Phyllis were in the hospital for two weeks. During that time there was a huge meeting at the shopping center for all the home owners. The Pravers asked if you wanted them to rebuild your house. I didn't know what else to do, so I said yes. You just had to sign a piece of paper and they rebuilt it. We rented a house in Grandview until it was finished.

Glen: I used to dream of my car. Oh, I was so proud of that thing. It only had about 15,000 miles on it and I had just put in a new radio. After I got out of the hospital I went up to look at it to see if I could pull the radio out. It just broke my heart. It was horribly beat up and the radio was gone.

Date 5/21/57

RESIDENT DISASTER CARD

Name WILLIAM H. GLENN Age 41

Address 7609 E. 110TH ST. - HICKMAN MILLS MO

Wife LORRAINE GLENN Age 35

Children CAROLYN LOUISE GLENN Age 7

DAVID BRUCE GLENN Age 5

Age

(List Injury or Death on BACK)

PERPETUAL MEMORIES

IX

People came back. As they moved into reconstructed houses the sounds of children, dogs, lawnmowers and laughter reclaimed those last long summer evenings. These were grateful sounds, celebrating life. Slowly, almost without notice, neighborhoods resumed their normal rhythm. Lives broken open began to mend over the deeply embedded memories, just as flesh healed over shards of embedded debris.

Our parents didn't talk about it much. It happened. It was no one's fault, no one could have stopped it, so the best thing to do was to clean up the mess and move on. Those resilient young couples, having grown up during the Depression or World War II, knew hardship and rebuilding. After all, they were just starting out, they could do it again. This time they were building more than a house. They were coming back to friends and a community. People who understood.

When we went back to school, into brand new classrooms, there were no counselors to talk to us about how we felt. Our teachers carefully avoided the subject, sensitive to the feelings of those children who had lost a parent or sibling. They never explained why the little girl in the second row of my third grade class slurred her words and seemed not to hear us, or how she had spent her summer in intensive care with severe head wounds. I remember only one reference made to May 20th. On the school bus I overheard a girl talking about the chemistry set her brother had received for his birthday that previous spring. She claimed that his experiments had resulted in the tornado. Taking the adult cue, we went back to talking about Elvis Presley or that new television show starting in September, *Leave It To Beaver*. But now when we played in the sandpile, instead of army men overrunning the villages, tornadoes swooped down out of our swinging arms to destroy the miniature houses we constructed out of all the scrap lumber lying around. These simple houses evolved into elaborate structures that we could change around at will. Our parents had helplessly watched while our houses were destroyed, but that wouldn't happen to the ones we made. We controlled their destiny.

In the real world, the storm cellars went in right away. Every block had several holes dug next to backyard patios. One opportunistic salesman sold ready-made concrete cylinders with a submarine-type ladder leading into them. They could be sunk right into a hole and held a family of six. Originally marketed for air raids, they became instant storm shelters. Perhaps anticipating that they would rise back up out of the ground within a few years, my father had a shelter poured, making an added patio. Over the years, many a tornado watch caused David and me to pack a suitcase full of our favorite things to have ready at the back door for a quick dash to the storm cellar. We spent many an evening in there with neighbors. Even those who had the instant cellars preferred the company of others during storms, and we gravitated to each other. After it was discovered that four families on our part of the block had spaghetti the night of the tornado, the ritualistic greeting when neighbors gathered in our shelter was, "All right, who had spaghetti tonight?" I remember those gatherings being like block parties. With churning skies overhead, out of sight, we visited and laughed, cocky enough to believe that another one wouldn't get us. We were survivors. But this bravura masked the nervousness and tension that none of us admitted to. Even as children, we knew the fear was just below the surface and our numbers and words held it at bay. After a while, as survivors moved away, these gatherings stopped. The new neighbors didn't see why we should all go to one place.

Many of us came back with new strength. The capriciousness of the tornado had determined our survival, leaving us feeling helpless and out of control. Accepting that challenge, we proved our ability to rebound. Now we knew we could face a crisis and carry on. In the years just after the tornado, a higher morale showed itself in community pride. In 1962 the Ruskin High School marching band was invited to the Rose Bowl Parade. While the announcers talked about the perseverance of a school district destroyed just five years before, the band could be heard playing its new theme song; "Rolling Thunder."

GORDON AND SHIRLEY GROSS
Shirley: We had a basement put in and always tried to let our immediate neighbors know when there were any storms, to tell them to come over. It was a totally different attitude. We really kept track of each other when there were storms.

Our bridge club was a pretty close-knit bunch of people anyway, but I think after the tornado we were closer. This group still gets together from all over the country and made a point to meet at the Presbyterian church's fortieth anniversary. That's a pretty tight bond, and it's still there. I don't know if it would have been that strong without the tornado.

We've always said that the tornado made a big difference in our lives in that really, from that day on we got over attachment to things, stuff you owned. Even now, when we come home from vacation our family joke is to say, "Well, the house is still here."

Gordon: I remember conversations about how the one thing the tornado did was make us realize that all that really counted was your family's safety. Everything else is just stuff that you can replace or forget.

We were all in our twenties and early thirties, so most of the men were recent veterans. We were trained to react to a situation. With that military background we thought, O.K., this is a mess, it's like war. We just switched to survivor mode. We saw to it everyone was taken care of, did what we did to get through it. Then it was back to work.

Shirley: Oddly enough, being in the tornado got me over my fear of them. I'm more able to look at them calmly now. I know I can actually survive one.

SHERYL JEPPESEN MCKINNEY

We lived with the tornado for years. It was a sore subject. Dad had twelve operations on his leg and it wasn't until 1971 that he could walk without a brace or cast. Many times we'd think it was healed and then it would break apart again. That meant a lot of the time he was out of work too. It just became a part of our lives growing up.

I ended up going to grade school at Burke. We would be dismissed at twelve-thirty or one if we were in a tornado watch. It happened a lot. We had good reason to be fearful. There was also a tornado plan if we were still at school. Two classrooms were assigned to a nearby house with a basement. But anytime there was a thunderstorm some of us got upset. Steve Johnston was in my first grade class. His father had been killed in the tornado and he was badly injured. So when there were storms, several of us in that class were shaking and crying.

You know, every time I go to Martin City it seems like there are storm warnings. Recently we were having dinner at the Smoke Stack Barbecue and a storm came up. My husband kept saying, "What's wrong with you?" But it just always brings it back again.

WALT BODINE

One thing the 1957 tornado did was make us realize how important it was to have a coordinated plan among the local hospitals. At the time, each hospital had its own method for handling any kind of wide scale trauma, but there were no special phone lines between hospitals. That's why Menorah was swamped with casualties while other hospitals waited for patients. After going through such a disaster, the medical community really knew what they had to work on, and the result was Kansas City now has a very good emergency system.

HELEN BOYLES

We're still together. Even the neighbors who have moved away keep in constant contact. The fact that we went through this tragedy together has kept us close.

We used to have tornado parties. Every year for a long time we'd get together at someone's house and bring a covered dish. As people moved away, they'd still come back for the party.

All of us were just beginning to get our houses the way we wanted them. We had a brand-new living room set and Libby's room was just done the way she liked it But when I saw all that destroyed, it didn't mean a thing. I think most of us were so darn glad we were alive, we didn't think about what we lost.

AUDREY GERRED BECKLEY

People who haven't been in one think we're crazy, and, of course, I've heard people complain about the warnings we get now. But I'd rather run for nothing than get caught.

MARIALICE ETEM

Things can go so fast, so they don't really count. All of a sudden you didn't care about anything you ever owned. What mattered was that we were all together.

MARJORIE MONTEE

When Mark started school his teacher told me that every time there was a stormy - looking cloud he'd get up out of his seat and watch the sky. Because he's deaf he was particularly vulnerable and determined that another tornado wouldn't surprise him.

JEAN HAYES

It made us aware of how devastating weather can be. Before the tornado we never considered the danger. If someone said there's a storm coming, you'd say, So what? After that, you paid attention. Now we are aware how it can affect you.

I don't think about it much anymore, but for a long, long time that was the only thing on your mind.

BETTY HAMBEL

The good part was we were alive. Everything else was replaceable. Your whole attitude changes. It's like God came down and slapped us around a little bit and said to straighten up. That was back in the days when everyone wanted a new house and new furniture. But then it was gone and we were thankful that we didn't lose more than we lost.

We were all new to the neighborhood, just starting to get acquainted. The tornado pulled us together real quick. Now, if there's a tornado warning or watch my kids and I call each other to make sure everyone knows. I still get squeamish just talking about it.

JEAN FROUNFELTER

It doesn't take you long to figure out that material possessions don't mean much. We lost things but they were replaceable. We had each other, and that was the main thing. It always is. It takes a very short time to be grateful to the tip of your toes. Then you go through the anguish of reassembling your home. That is agonizing, but it's something you know how to do. You've done it before and you can do it again. After all, this was our little chunk of Missouri. When our house was blown away we didn't run. We said, "Lordy, you know it isn't going to happen to us again." So we had it all built back.

We wanted to be back with the same neighbors. There's a camaraderie that goes along with that kind of experience. We were a part of each other's stories. We couldn't wait to have a block party and celebrate that we were still here, by golly.

BLAINE STECK

This shook a lot of people up. It could happen to us. Prior to this, no one thought too much about it. The next school year at Burke, and the first year in the rebuilt high school, we had tornado drills. I can still remember having those drills and hearing the sound of that siren. We'd go to our designated area in the locker rooms and I'd hear high school kids crying. You know how kids are during drills — kind of boisterous and fooling around. But I'll tell you, there for several years when they heard that siren they didn't say a word, they didn't do anything. They cried. Boy, I had a bunch of them that cried. You just wouldn't think it would affect them like that, but it did.

All those houses out there were gone and people really had to re-make their lives. That was reality, you had to face up to that. I think the people out there came closer together and instilled in each other that there was a future. People did build back. Everything worked out, but it took a lot of effort on everyone's part.

MARJORIE LANGFORD

The first time we had a tornado alert that next school year, I left my office, went out to my car, and came home. I didn't tell anyone I was leaving the building. All of a sudden here I was, at home. I went back to school later, but I just wanted to be at home.

Your priorities change when you've been through something like that. You find that some of the things you thought were important aren't. You have to give up some control. No matter how much insurance you have, or how careful you are, you realize you're not in charge.

TREVA WOODLING

After the tornado, at first I said I wasn't going to move back there. But then I thought you might not be at home when it hit. You could be anywhere, so you can't move away from them.

We were petrified every time there was a storm. Diane was scared every time it rained and when she heard a train. After I was paralyzed, I made up my mind I wasn't going to leave the house during storms. We left the house once and look what happened.

I don't know, maybe I'm wrong, but I felt sometimes like the tornado happened to show people that materialistic things don't mean anything and to maybe straighten up our lives. Not that Harry and I had been bad people, because we hadn't. But there were times I felt maybe these things happen to let people know how they should live.

Disasters do bring people close together, the tornado brought us closer to people. As much loss as we suffered, it didn't make us lose our faith in people or in God.

They called it an act of God. I don't know whether God let it happen. I don't know how anyone could know that. I do know we suffered terrible grief because of it, and that we received great love from people too. It makes you kind of stop and wonder.

AGGIE TURNBAUGH

A lot of the people who faced all that adversity went on to become civic leaders and prominent citizens. Just in our Jaycees we ended up with a state senator and a federal prosecuting attorney. Those Jaycees and their wives who worked together through that disaster have been our life-long friends. There was an indomitable spirit about the people. It was a beautiful example of what can come out of chaos, how people rally around each other. Surprisingly, it was people in their late twenties that stood up and did the pulling together to rebuild. Of course, most of them were vets too, and they'd been through things like that and I think that kind of helped too. They had faced devastation during the war and that served the area in good stead.

There were a lot of stories that were missed as we reported the aftermath, things people were doing to help. No one thought they were heroes. No one made a big deal about what they did, they just did it, and didn't want to tell us about it.

On September 19 the Hickman Mills Chamber of Commerce gave a dinner of thanks in the brand-new high school gymnasium. Along with the Optimist Club of Ruskin Heights-Hickman Mills, the Hickman Mills American Legion Post, the Hickman Mills Lions Club and the School Board of Consolidated School District #1, their purpose was to "publicly recognize the valiant and tireless efforts of individuals and organizations from without our community, and to express our heartfelt gratitude for the assistance received from them as a result of those efforts, following the giant tornado of May 20, 1957."

The evening started with a motor tour of the disaster area. After a roast beef dinner, there was a short film, "Disaster At Twilight," juxtaposing the devastation with the largely rebuilt community.

Twenty-one awards were presented by Russ Millin, then president of the Hickman Mills Chamber of Commerce, to organizations

as diverse as the Mennonite Disaster Service and the Missouri High-
way Patrol. Guests, including Harry Truman, Governor James Blair
and Mayor Bartle, enjoyed their fudge cake and coffee as Senator
Stuart Symington brought the evening to a close with his com-
ments. The path widened that night, embracing all those who made
healing possible.

JEAN HENDERSHOT

I get put out with people who pay no attention to tornado warnings. Especially now that we have such good ways of detecting them.

DR. GRACE KETTERMAN

I started my pediatrics practice at the Hickman Mills clinic that
fall. I listened to a lot of parents talking about their children's nightmares—and their own, for that matter. Frequently they told me their
children woke up screaming, or that they were terrified of even regular
thunderstorms. Since I lived through that night with them I certainly
understood why, but I told them the best way to help their children
get over the fear was to talk about it. I suggested that families sit
down together and talk about what they remembered and what part
still frightened them. I don't know how many families actually did
that. It was a time in our culture when fears weren't openly dis-
cussed much.

WILLIS AND MAXINE WATKINS

Maxine: Every time it got stormy after that you'd look out and the
whole neighborhood would be watching the sky.
Willis: Our seven-year-old daughter was pretty upset when it started
thundering and lightning. She and the other kids would gather up
their treasures and head for the basement.
Maxine: You could always tell what was their most precious possession at that time. They'd get so busy, they'd forget about the
storm. Then they'd have to carry it all back.

JOE KRAMER

In the aftermath, the community did seem to pull together and
acquire a sense of unity and purpose. The Homes Association was
actually the only authority out there, since it wasn't part of Kansas
City yet. The county was too large to be effective in all the immediate local problems that arose. They were great for police and needs

like that, but county government didn't know the individuals like the Homes Association people did. It produced a community spirit I had never noticed before.

JEAN MCCOY

Right after it was over you didn't care a thing about material possessions. That just didn't seem to matter when you heard about and saw other families who had members badly injured or killed. You just felt fortunate to be alive.

We were a really close neighborhood. None of us had lived there very long, and most of us stayed for years, so having that tornado experience early in our relationship really bonded us together. Our kids were all the same age, our husbands were all GIs and sort of in the same boat buying our first home. Our kids went to school together and played ball together, but even with all those things in common, the underlining thread was that we had survived together.

MARY NORTHCRAFT

I think I'm O.K. until I hear the alarms go off, and then I'm not. People say, Oh they put that alarm off all the time and they shouldn't because they scare people needlessly. But I think, you haven't been through one.

DOROTHY KOTSIFAKIS

Every year we had a block-party picnic to commemorate the tornado, and every time there was a big storm. We'd disband real quick, and finally we said, "Hey, we're drawing them. Let's quit this."

The next summer we stayed in a little cabin near Denver, next to a railroad track. In the middle of the night the kids would hear those trains and think they were going through it again. It took the kids a long time to get over it. They woke up screaming many nights.

GLEN AND JEAN WILLIAMS

Jean: Every year I always think, if we make it past May 20th we'll be O.K. storm-wise. I don't know why, because you can have storms any time of the year. But I remember it every year. Whenever those spring storms start blowing hard it makes me kind of nervous still.
Glen: If you're in a car wreck you get back in a car again. We figured there was no reason to move out of the house. We have a healthy respect for storms and we go to the basement, but it didn't scare us

away. But the people who laugh at us for taking precautions really irritate me.

With all the bad that was happening with this thing, you discovered that there is a lot of good in people. You really do. I couldn't forget all the help the people at our church gave us. I didn't belong to our church at the time, but while I was twirling around in that funnel I said, "God, if you can get me out of this thing I'm going to join the church." It shook the hell out of me.

SIDNEY BATES

There was a boy in the high school band with me the next year whose mother and sister had been killed. I remember being very careful around him for a while, always watching what I said. I was aware of his particular wounds and didn't want to open them.

My brother was a senior that next year and I seem to remember something about putting a picture of a tornado inside the class ring. It was the jeweler's idea, but the students and staff thought it was a tasteless one.

Almost everyone at school that next year had been affected by the tornado, so there was no need to discuss it. It was such a universal experience for my friends and their families that it became part of our culture. It was just there, we didn't need to talk about it.

DONNA BRAMBLE WILLIAMS

The tornado gave me a tremendous respect for life. With all the health problems it caused for my family, I could have let it consume me. But I always figured God put me here for a purpose, and it wasn't to be bitter. I never experienced those wild teenage years because I had gone through enough injuries already and knew how easily lives could be changed forever. There was so much suffering and pain around me through those years that it made me a much more compassionate person.

ANNA LEE HEMBREE

Our homes were gone, the neighborhood destroyed physically, and I was so afraid that the people wouldn't come back. But the neighborhood was far more than just houses. Everyone did return and for that reason we rejoiced.

The next spring, a cornstalk grew in our side yard, an unexpected gift from some Kansas farm along the tornado's path. But we didn't need strange plants to remind us that tornado season was on us again. In March, the sirens went in near all the schools, and while their presence comforted us, we dreaded their sound. We were again more aware of the sound of trains, and during stormy times let out a tense breath every time we heard the locomotive's whistle. It was going to be a tough spring to get through without some acknowledgment of what we had all been through since last May. People still weren't anxious to talk about that night, but they needed ceremony to resolve their experience.

They got that chance on a hot bright Sunday afternoon just two days short of the first anniversary. A brick memorial along Blue Ridge just south of the high school, at the entryway of the Ruskin development, stood as a symbol of courage and sacrifice. At its presentation that day, the community leaders simply dedicated the memorial to those who had lost their lives. Three windows at the top of the structure represented faith, hope and love. They reminded us all of how we had "found the will and spiritual strength to build anew." The tornado's force was spent, but its power held us in time.

**Senator Stuart Symington
at the
Memorial Dedication**

SOURCE NOTES

PART ONE

1. PATH'S BEGINNING

2. John Steuart Curry painting, *Tornado* : *World Book Encyclopedia*, Volume 13, 1953.
2. Joe Audsley: Interview, February 23, 1995.
2. located in Kansas City: *Time*, June 27, 1955.
2. Tornadoes in a single month: *Science News Letter*, June 22, 1957.
2. First tornado of the day: John G. Fuller, *Tornado Watch #211*, 54-55.
3. Founded as a trading post: *History of Jackson County*, 358.
3. Truman helping: Stephen S. Slaughter, *History of a Missouri Farm Family*, 72.
3. Threshing crews: David McCullough, *Truman*, 78.
3. Treva Woodling: Interview, February 20, 1996.
3. kindergarten class: Interview, Tim Nichols, November 7, 1994.
3. Blaine Steck: Interview, December 13, 1994.
3. Dr. Alexander Shifrin: Interview February 23, 1996.
4. danger of tornadic activity: Interview, Joe Audsley, February 23, 1995.
4. A's starting lineup: *Kansas City Times*, May 20, 1957, 1.
4. *I Love Lucy* : *Kansas City Times*, May 20, 1957, 23.
4. surface air rises: *Tornado Formation,* NSSFC brochure.
4. hydrogen bomb: John G. Fuller, *Tornado #211*, 11-12.
5. 1879 Lee's Summit tornado: *History of Jackson County*, 89.
5. 1946 Martin City tornado: *Kansas City Times*, May 24, 1946, 1.
5. worst damage: *Kansas City Times*, May 24, 1946, 1.
5. 1879, 86 miles: *Kansas City Tornadoes*, NSFC, 4.
5. 1946, ten miles: *Kansas City Times*, May 24, 1946, 1.
5. Whitely estate: *Kansas City Star*, January 25, 1953, 18.
5. half-acre lots: Interview, Marjorie Langford, February 3, 1995.
6. Levittown: David Halberstam, *The Fifties* , 132-135.

6.   housing starts: William Manchester, *The Glory and the Dream,*

7.   community of Ruskin Heights: Interview, Lou Davis, September 20, 1995.

7.   go to school?: Interview, Marjorie Langford, February 3, 1995.

7.   opened its doors: *Kansas City Star,* January 28, 1969.

7.   new Ruskin High School: Interview, Blaine Steck, December 13, 1994.

7.   Burke and Truman: Interview, Joe Nesbit, May 5, 1995.

7.   enrollment jumped: Consolidated School District brochure, 1957.

8.   Sam Walton: Vance H. Trimble, *Sam Walton: Founder of Wal-Mart* , 73.

8.   Presiding Judge: David McCullough, *Truman,* 176-177.

2. "Look At This Cloud"

11.   long day: Interview, Marjorie Langford, February 3, 1995.

11.   Crest Drive-In: *Kansas City Times,* May 20, 1957.

11.   thrill of performance: *Kansas City Star,* May 19,1957, 20A.

11.   Gene Montee: Interview, May 23, 1995.

11.   Jean McCoy: Interview, April 24, 1995.

11.   Mary Northcraft: Interview, April 27, 1995.

12.   Helen Boyles: Interview, March 29, 1995.

12.   Joe Audsley: Interview, February 23, 1995.

12.   "Radar at the Kansas City weather bureau": NSSFC media transcripts.

12.   Vietnam: *Kansas City Star,* May 20, 1957, 5.

12.   "Peanuts": *Kansas City Times* , May 20, 1957, 22.

13.   "east of the city": NSSFC media transcripts.

13.   Darryl Haynes: Walt Bodine, *Diary of a Disaster,* WDAF radio, May 1957.

13.   Walt Bodine: Interview, February 2, 1996.

13.   Marjorie Langford: Interview, February 2, 1995.

14.   Stanley Jeppsen: Interview, October 12, 1995.

14.   Sheryl Jeppsen McKinney: Interview, October 28, 1995.

15.   Charlie Cook: Interview, February 2, 1996.

15.   Norman Caron: Interview, September 19, 1996.

16.   Clyde Renken: Interview May 1, 1995.

16.   Jim and Aggie Turnbaugh: Interview, September 21, 1995.

17.   Willis and Maxine Watkins: Interview, April 7, 1995.

17.   Pete and Dorothy Kotsifakis: Interview, May 16, 1995.

18.   Judy Jones Heckadon: Interview, May 2, 1996.
18.   Elinor Steinbrueck: Interview, October 2, 1995.
19.   Donna Bramble Williams: Interview, November 4, 1995.
19.   George Moore: Interview, March 31, 1995.
19.   Gene and Marjorie Montee: Interview, May 23, 1995.
20.   Charles Gray: Interview, February 27, 1996.
20.   Mike Angotti: Interview, May 6, 1996.
20.   Sidney Bates: Interview, February 27, 1996.
21.   Blaine Steck: Interview, December 13, 1994.
21.   Audrey Gerred Beckley: Interview, February 15,1996.
21.   Helen Boyles: Interview, March 29, 1995.
22.   Russ Millin: Interview, January 28, 1995.
22.   Janie Killion: Interview, May 14, 1995.
22.   Jeanne Johnston Gorman: Interview, October 13, 1994.
23.   Art and Ernestine Peterson: Interview, November 3, 1994.
23.   Betty Hambel: Interview, October 28, 1994.
23.   Roy and Thelma Kirkman: Interview, October 11, 1994.
24.   Albert Caudle: Interview, January 20, 1995.
24.   Rev. Harry Dale Collier: Interview (letter), June 10, 1995.
24.   Diane Nehring LeValley: Interview, May 2, 1996.
25.   Dean Evans: Interview, October 9, 1995.
25.   Treva Woodling: Interview, February 20, 1996.
26.   Herb and Edna Green: Interview, November 18, 1994.
27.   Joe Kramer: Interview, April 6, 1995.
27.   Leon Felson: Walt Bodine, *Diary of a Disaster*, WDAF radio, May 1957.
27.   Jean Hendershot: Interview, March 3, 1995.
28.   Steve Galler: Interview, January 8, 1995.
28.   Peggy McNamara: Interview, November 8, 1994.
28.   Jean Hayes: Interview, October 3, 1994.
29.   Myrna Smith: Interview, February 6, 1995.
29.   Paul and Jane Potter: Interview, October 6, 1994.
30.   E.J. and Jean Frounfelter: Interview, November 10, 1994.
30.   Clyde Ofner Jr.: Interview, February 12, 1996.
30.   Jean McCoy: Interview, April 24, 1995.
31.   Dolores Schuenemeyer: Interview, February 13, 1996
31.   Gordan and Shirley Gross: Interview, November 3, 1995.
32.   Bill Martin: Interview, April 10, 1995.
32.   Glen and Jean Williams: Interview, December 8, 1994.
33.   Bill McCarty: Interview, March 6, 1995.
33.   Austin Shute: Interview, February 16, 1995.

3. Like A Thousand Jets

35. Bob Babb: Walt Bodine, *Diary of a Disaster*, WDAF radio, May 1957.
36. Ruth Ray: Interview, November 14, 1994.
36. Stanley Jeppesen: Interview, October 12, 1995.
36. Gene and Marjorie Montee: Interview, May 23, 1995.
37. Clyde Renken: Interview, May 1, 1995.
37. Robert Jackson: Stuart G. Bigler, *Weatherwise,* June 1958, 88-90.
38. Marialice Etem: Interview, May 30, 1995.
38. Elinor Steinbrueck: Interview, October 2, 1995.
39. Marjorie Langford: Interview, February 3, 1995.
39. Willis Watkins: Interview, April 7, 1995.
39. Pete Kotsifakis: Interview, May 16, 1995.
39. Anna Lee Hembree: Interview, May 16, 1995.
39. Marta Schmacher: Interview, May 16, 1995.
40. Judy Jones Heckadon: Interview, May 2, 1996.
40. Donna Bramble Williams: Interview, November 4, 1995.
40. Loren Gaydusek: Interview, May 31,1995.
40. Mike Angotti: Interview, May 6, 1996.
41. Thelma Kirkman: Interview, October 11, 1994.
41. Betty Hambel: Interview, October 28, 1994.
41. Johnie Eager: Interview, January 26, 1995.
41. Al Caudle: Interview, January 20, 1995.
42. Treva Woodling: Interview, February 20, 1996.
42. Rev. Loren Goings: Interview May 1, 1995.
43. Blaine Steck: Interview, December 13, 1994.
43. Diane Nehring LeValley: Interview, May 2, 1996.
43. Audrey Gerred Beckley: Interview, February 15, 1996.
44. Helen Boyles: Interview, March 29, 1995.
44. Louis Mannen: Interview, March 22, 1996.
44. Pat Jardes: Interview, April 20, 1995.
44. Jean Hayes: Interview, October 3, 1994.
45. Steve Galler: Interview, January 8, 1995.
45. Dana Galler Corder: Interview, October 27, 1994.
45. Pam Potter Smith: Interview, October 21, 1994.
45. Carol Hayes: Interview, October 21, 1994.
45. Peggy McNamara: Interview, November 8, 1994.
46. David Millin: Interview, January 29, 1995.
46. Dean and Nancy Evans: Interview, October 9, 1995.
46. Jean Frounfelter: Interview, November 10, 1994.
47. Glen and Jean Williams: Interview, December 8, 1994.
47. Mary Northcraft: Interview, April 27, 1995.
47. Jean McCoy: Interview, April 24, 1995.

47.   James Shoot: Interview, January 29, 1995.
48.   Richard McMillin: Walt Bodine, *Diary of a Disaster*, WDAF radio, May 1957.
48.   Bill Martin: Interview, April 10, 1995.

4. Last People On Earth

50.   Stanley Jeppesen: Interview, October 12, 1995.
50.   Sheryl Jeppesen McKinney: Interview, November 14, 1995.
51.   Charlie Cook: Interview, February 2, 1996.
52.   Norman Caron: Interview, September 19, 1996.
52.   Jim and Aggie Turnbaugh: Interview, September 21, 1995.
53.   Walt Bodine: Interview, February 1, 1996.
53.   Russ Millin: Interview, January 28, 1995.
54.   David Millin: Interview, January 29, 1995.
55.   Ruth Ray: Interview, November 14, 1994.
55.   Dr. Alexander Shifrin: Interview, February 23, 1996.
55.   Willis Watkins: Interview, April 7, 1995.
56.   Clyde Renken: Interview, May 1, 1995.
57.   Joe Nesbit: Interview May 5, 1995.
57.   Sidney Bates: Interview, February 27, 1996.
58.   Loren Gaydusek: Interview, May 31, 1995.
58.   Marjorie Langford: Interview, February 3, 1995.
59.   Marialice Etem: Interview, May 30, 1995.
60.   Pete and Dorothy Kotsifakis: Interview, May 16, 1995.
61.   Anna Lee Hembree: Interview, May 16, 1995.
61.   Marta Schumacher: Interview, May 16, 1995.
62.   Judy Jones Heckadon: Interview, May 2, 1996.
62.   Donna Bramble Williams: Interview, November 4, 1995.
62.   Gene and Marjorie Montee: Interview, May 23, 1995.
64.   Mike Angotti: Interview, May 6, 1996.
64.   Johnie and Bill Eager: Interview, January 26, 1995, October 30, 1995.
65.   authorization to drive: Walt Bodine, *Diary of a Disaster*, WDAF radio, May 1957.
65.   transport the injured: IBID
66.   frantic edge of his voice: IBID
66.   "No one is moving": IBID
66.   that it was gone: IBID
66.   Charles Gray: Interview, February 27, 1996.
67.   Blaine Steck: Interview, December 13, 1994.
67.   Audrey Gerred Beckley: Interview, February 15, 1996.

69. Diane Nehring LeValley: Interview, May 2, 1996.
69. Al Caudle: Interview, January 20, 1995.
70. "For God's sake do so": Congressional Report, July 1957.
70. Rev. Harry Dale Collier: Interview (letter), June 10, 1995.
71. Treva Woodling: Interview, February 20, 1996.
72. Louis Mannen: Interview, March 22, 1996.
72. Helen Boyles: Interview, March 29, 1995.
73. Leon Felson: Walt Bodine, *Diary of a Disaster*, WDAF radio, May 1957.
73. Jean Hayes: Interview, October 3, 1994.
74. Carol Hayes: Interview, October 21, 1994.
75. Peggy McNamara: Interview,   November 8, 1994.
75. Paul Potter: Interview, October 6, 1994.
76. Betty Hambel: Interview, October 28, 1994.
77. Leon Felson: Walt Bodine, *Diary of a Disaster*, WDAF radio, May 1957.
77. Jack Brams: IBID
78. Dean and Nancy Evans: Interview, October 9, 1995.
79. Rev. Loren Goings: Interview, May 1, 1995.
79. Bill and Norma Martin: Interview, April 10, 1995.
80. Jeanne Johnston Gorman: Interview, October 13, 1994.
81. E.J. and Jean Frounfelter: Interview, Novemeber 10, 1994.
82. Clyde Ofner Jr.: Interview, February 12, 1996.
82. Joe Kramer: Interview, April 6, 1995.
83. Leon Felson: Walt Bodine, *Diary of a Disaster*, WDAF radio, May 1957.
84. Sister Michaela Marie: IBID
84. Helen Eimer: IBID
84. Bob and Jean McCoy: Interview, April 24, 1995.
85. Bill and May Northcraft: Interview, April 27, 1995.
86. Dolores Schunemeyer: Interview, February 13, 1996.
86. Bill Leeds: Walt Bodine, *Diary of a Disaster*, WDAF radio, May 1957.
86. Norman Caron: Interview, September 19,1996.
87. Shirley Gross: Interview, November 13, 1995.
87. Teresa Kirschbaum: Interview, October 25, 1994.
88. "overjoyed to see them": Bill Glenn, letter to relatives, May 27, 1957.
89. Jean Hendershot: Interview, March 3, 1995.
89. Austin Shute: Interview, February 16, 1995.
89. Meryl Ostergard: Interview, April 13, 1995.
90. "This is an urgent appeal": Walt Bodine, *Diary of a Disaster*, WDAF radio, 5/57.
91. Grace Ketterman: Interview, May 6, 1995.
91. Glen and Jean Williams: Interview, December 8, 1994.

92. Treva Woodling: Interview, February 20, 1996.
93. Walt Bodine: Interview, February 1, 1996.
93. hoarse dispatcher: Walt Bodine, *Diary of a Disaster*, WDAF radio, May 1957.
93. Leon Felson: IBID
93. Bob Babb: IBID
94. Joe Audsley: Interview, February 23, 1995.

5. You Laugh To Survive

95. teenage boys: Interview, Bill Eager, October 30, 1995.
95. looked like it had been sodded: Al Caudle, Interview, January 20, 1995.
95. closet door: Myrna Smith, Interview (letter) February 2, 1995.
95. clothing that did survive: Mary Alice Etem, Interview, May 30, 1995.
95. no one understood: Jean Frounfelter, Interview, November 10, 1994.
95. "milk man": Jim and Aggie Turnbaugh, *Twilight Twister*, June 1957.
95. "Gone With the Wind": Jean Frounfelter, Interview, November 10, 1994.
95. "Here Lies Our Mortage": Betty Hambel, Interview, October 28, 1994.
95. "All Shook Up": Jean McCoy, Interview, April 24, 1995.
96. decorating their trees": Gary Nelson, Interview, January 4, 1995.
96. Pete and Dorothy Kotsifakis: Interview, May 16, 1995.
97. Marta Schumacher: Interview, May 16, 1995.
97. Anna Lee Hambree: Interview, May 16, 1995.
97. Judy Jones Heckadon: Interview, May 2, 1996.
97. Clyde Renken: Interview, May 1, 1995.
98. Stanley Jeppesen: Interview, October 12, 1995.
98. Dean Evans: Interview, October 9, 1995.
98. Gene and Marjorie Montee: Interview, May 23, 1995.
98. Diane Nehring LeValley: Interview, May 2, 1996.
99. Herb and Edna Green: Interview, November 11, 1994.
99. Jean Hayes: Interview, October 3, 1994.
99. Paul and Jane Potter: Interview, October 6, 1994.
100. Roy and Thelma Kirkman: Interview, October 11, 1994.
100. Betty Hambel: Interview, October 28, 1994.
101. Treva Woodling: Interview, February 20, 1996.
101. Louis Mannen: Interview, March 22, 1996.

101.	Jean Williams: Interview, December 8, 1994.
101.	Blaine Steck: Interview, December 13, 1994.
101.	Austin Shute: Interview, February 16, 1995.
101.	Bill and Mary Northcraft: Interview, April 27, 1995.
102.	Helen Boyles: Interview, March 29, 1995.
102.	Pat Jardes: Interview, April 20, 1995.
102.	Bill and Greg McCarty: Interview, January 26, 1995, March 6, 1995.
102.	E.J. and Jean Frounfelter: Interview, November 10, 1994.
104.	Aggie Turnbaugh: Interview, September 21, 1995.

PART TWO

6. Tracked By The Cisco Kid

105.	path of 71miles: Richard J. Williams, *Kansas City Tornadoes* , 1984.
105.	moving 42 miles per hour: IBID
105.	winds up to 500mph,: *Kansas City Times,* May 22,2957, 1.
105.	eyewitness reports: *Kansas City Times* ,May 21, 1957, 1.
105.	footage for *Today* : Interview, Walt Bodine, February 1, 1996.
105.	NBC radio: IBID
105.	Claude Dorsey: Interview, May 31, 1995.
105.	Joe Kramer: Interview, April 6, 1995.
105.	Charles Gray: Interview, February 27, 1996.
105.	first lives: *Kansas City Times* , May 21, 1.
105.	found in a field: IBID
106.	range of destruction: *Kansas City Star* , May 21, 1957, 1.
106.	business along Main Street: Jim and Aggie Turnbaugh, *Twilight Twister,* 6/57.
106.	only good news: *Jackson County Advocate* , May 23, 1957.
106.	residents of the Ozanam: IBID
106.	Jess and Jim's: IBID
106.	Truman Corners: IBID
106.	Hickman Mills: *Kansas City Star* , May 21, 1957, 2.
106.	pink dress: *Kansas City Times* , May 21, 1957, 1A.
107.	larger tornado: *Kansas City Times* , May 22, 1957, 2.
107.	Sibley:*Kansas City Times* , May 21, 1957.
107.	water tower held: *Jackson County Advocate* , May 30, 1957.
107.	minus the song: IBID

107.   "Let her blow": Interview, Loren Goings, May 1, 1995.
107.   caught in the shower: Interview, Thelma Kirkman, October 11, 1994.
107.   Father Micheal Lynch: *Jackson County Advocate*, May 30, 1957.
107.   Edith Dixon: *Kansas City Star*, July 5, 1957, 19A.
109.   Joe Audsley: Interview February 23, 1995.
109.   Walt Bodine: Interview, February 1, 1996.
110.   Jim and Aggie Trunbaugh: Interview, September 21, 1995.
112.   Willis Watkins: Interview, April 7, 1995.
112.   Josephine Renken: Interview, May 1, 1995.
112.   Pete Kotsifakis: Interview, May 16, 1995.
112.   Sidney Bates: Interview, February 27, 1996.
113.   Dean Evans: Interview, October 9, 1995.
113.   Clyde Ofner Jr.: Interview, February 12, 1996.
114.   Donna Bramble Williams: Interview, November 4, 1995.
114.   Helen Boyles: Interview, March 29, 1995.
115.   Audrey Gerred Beckley: Interview, February 15, 1996.
115.   Lou Davis: Interview, September 20, 1995.
116.   Treva Woodling: Interview, February 20, 1996.
116.   Charlie Cook: Interview, February 2, 1996.
117.   Diane Nehring LeValley: Interview, May 2, 1996.
117.   Jean Hayes: Interview, Octoer 3, 1994.
117.   Carol Hayes: Interview, October 21, 1994.
118.   Dana Galler Corder: Interview, October 27, 1994.
118.   Mike McNamara: Interview, November 15, 1994.
118.   Blaine Steck: Interview, December 13, 1994.
118.   Bill Eager: Interview, October 30, 1995.
118.   Russ Millin: Interview, January 28, 1995.
119.   Gene Montee: Interview, May 23, 1995.
119.   Thelma Kirkman: Interview, October 11, 1994.
119.   Charles Gray: Interview, February 27, 1996.
120.   Betty Hambel: Interview, October 28, 1994.
120.   Herb Green: Interview, November 18, 1994.
120.   Jean Frounfelter: Interview, November 10, 1994.
121.   Jean Hendershot: Interview, March 3, 1995.
121.   Austin Shute: Interview, February 16, 1995.
121.   Shirley Gross: Interview, November 3, 1995.
122.   Joe Kramer: Interview, April 6, 1995.
123.   Bill Martin: Interview, April 10, 1995.
123.   Loren Goings: Interview, May 1, 1995.
123.   Joe Nesbit: Interview, May 5, 1995.
124.   Jean McCoy: Interview, April 24, 1995.
124.   Mary Northcraft: Interview, April 27, 1995.
124.   Glen Williams: Interview, December 8, 1994.

7. When Ford Shakes Hands With Chevy

125. "Here's cooperation": *Jackson County Advocate*, May 23, 1957, 8.
125. by the time: *Kansas City Times*, May 21, 1957, 1.
125. thirty dozen eggs: *Kansas City Star*, May 22, 1957.
125. Parke Davis: *Kansas City Star*, May 22, 1957.
125. Salyers Prescription Shop: *Jackson County Advocate*, May 23, 1957.
125. Rainen Furniture: *Kansas City Star*, May 22, 1957, 24.
126. Milgram's: *Kansas City Times*, May 22, 1957.
126. placed notices: *City Star*, May 23, 1957.
126. Grandview Bank: *Jackson County Advocate*, May 23, 1957.
126. one little girl: *Kansas City Star*, May 24, 1957.
126. Bruce School: *Kansas City Star*, May 22, 1957, 6.
126. Hogan High School: *Kansas Cityt Times*, May 24, 1957.
126. theater night: *Kansas City Star*, June 3, 1957.
126. girl scout troop: *Jackson County Advocate*, June 27, 1957, 1.
126. Harry Truman spoke: *Kansas City Times*, May 22, 1957, 3.
127. Jim and Aggie Turnbaugh: Interview, September 21, 1995.
128. Stanley Jeppesen: Interview, October 12, 1995.
128. George Moore: Interview, March 31, 1995.
128. Elinor Steinbruck: Interview, October 2, 1995.
128. Pete Kotsifakis: Interview, May 16, 1995.
129. Ken Marley: Interview, October 15, 1995.
129. Clyde Renken: Interview, May 1, 1995.
130. Rev. Loren Goings: Interview, May 1, 1995.
130. Alice Hons: Interview, February 6, 1995.
131. Howard Massey: Interview, Novemeber 9, 1995.
131. Thelma Kirkman: Interview, October 11, 1995.
131. Jeanne Johnston Gorman: Interview, October 13, 1995.
132. Paul Potter: Interview, October 6, 1994.
132. Betty Hambel: Interview, October 28, 1994.
132. Herb Green: Interview, November 18, 1994.
133. Lucille Motsinger: Interview, February 11,1995.
133. Marjorie Langford: Interview, February 3, 1995.
133. Audrey Gerred Beckley: Interview, February 15, 199
134. Treva Woodling: Interview, February 20, 1996.
134. Peggy McNamara: Interview, November 8, 1994.
135. Nancy Evans: Interview, October 9, 1995.
135. Jean Hendershot: Interview, March 3, 1995.
135. Austin Shute: Interview, February 16, 1995.
135. Shirley Gross: Interview, November 3, 1995.

135. Clyde Ofner Jr.: Interview, February 12, 1996.
136. Bill McCarty: Interview, March 6, 1995.
136. Bob And Jean McCoy: Interview, April 24, 1995.
136. Bill and Mary Northcraft: Interview, April 27, 1995.
136. E.J. and Jean Frounfelter: Interview, November 10, 1995.
137. Glen and Jean Williams: Interview, December 8, 1994.
138. Joe Nesbit: Interview, May 5, 1995.
138. Louis Mannen: Interview, March 22, 1996.
139. Helen Boyles: Interview, March 29, 1995.
139. Sidney Bates: Interview, February 27, 1996.
139. Charles Gray: Interview, February 17, 1996.
139. Kramer: Interview, April 6, 1995.

8. A Symbol Of Hope

141. May 20, 1956: Harry Dale Collier, *History of the Ruskin Presbyterian Church*, '94.
141. Mass Meeting: Mass Meeting Notes May 25, 1957.
141. carpenter's strike: *Jackson County Advocate*, June 6, 1957.
142. first family: *Kansas City Star*, June 19, 1957, 1.
142. last to leave: *Kansas City Star*, September 26, 1957.
142. set up rock and roll: *Jackson County Advocate*, June 6, 1957.
142. "New Terror In A Savage Spring": *Life*, June 3, 1957, 27-33.
142. "Caught in the Suburbs": *Time*, June 3, 1957, 17,18.
142. "Sometimes It Boils Over": *Saturday Review*, October 4, 1958, 44.45.
142. "The Resurrection of Ruskin Heights": Jackson Lewis, *American Mercury*, January 1959, 112-116.
143. William Peck on "Houseparty": *Jackson County Advocate*, June 6, 1957.
143. Jim Turnbaugh: Interview, September 21, 1995.
143. Stanley Jeppesen: Interview, October 12, 1995.
144. Sheryl Jeppesen McKinney: Interview, November 14, 1995.
144. Elinor Steinbruck: Interview, October 2, 1995.
145. Loren Gaydusek: Interview, May 31, 1995.
145. Marialice Etem: Interview, May 30, 1996.
145. Willis and Maxine Watkins: Interview, April 7, 1995.
145. Walt Bodine: Interview, February 1, 1996.
146. Rev. Loren Goings: Interview, May 1, 1995.

9.   Perpetual Memories

167.   Jean Frounfelter: Interview, November 10, 1994.
168.   Blaine Steck: Interview, December 13, 1994.
168.   Marjorie Langford: Interview,February 3, 1995.
168.   Treva Woodling: Interview, February 20, 1996.
169.   Aggie Turnbaugh: Interview, September 21, 1995.
169.   dinner of thanks: Dinner Program, September 19, 1957.
170.   Jean Hendershot: Interview, March 3, 1995.
170.   Dr. Grace Ketterman: Interview, May 6, 1995.
170.   Willis and Maxine Watkins: Interview, April 7, 1995.
170.   Joe Kramer: Interview, April 6, 1995.
171.   Jean McCoy: Interview, April 24, 1995.
171.   Mary Northcraft: Interview, April 27, 1995.
171.   Dorothy Kotsifakis: Interview, May 16, 1995.
171.   Glen and Jean Williams: Interview, December 8, 1994.
172.   Sidney Bates: Interview, February 27, 1996.
172.   Donna Bramble Williams: Interview, November 4, 1995.
172.   Anna Lee Hembree: Interview, May 16, 1995.
173.   "found the will": Memorial Dedication Program, May 18, 1958.

BIBLIOGRAPHY

BOOKS

History of Jackson County. Jackson County, Missouri: Union Historical Company, 1881.

A History of Spring Hill, Kansas. Spring Hill, Kansas: Methodist Church, 1983.

Ballou, M.E. *Official Report on the Resources and Opportunities of Jackson County Missouri*. Jackson County: Jackson County Chamber of Commerce, 1926.

Fuller, John G. *Tornado Watch #211*. New York: William Morrow and Company, Inc., 1987.

Gordon, Lois and Alan. *American Chronicle*. New York: Atheneum, 1987.

Halberstam, David. *The Fifties.* New York: Villard Books, 1993.

Hamric, Sharon. *"...Like The Devil"*. Wichita, Kansas: Wichita Eagle and Beacon Publishing Company, 1991.

Manchester, William. *The Glory and the Dream: Volume Two* Boston: Little, Brown and Company, 1973.

McCullough, David. *Truman* . New York: Simon and Schuster Touchstone, 1992.

Scott, Mrs. Harry Sr.
Slaughter, Mrs. J.M. *History of the Hickman Mills Community Christian Church.* Pennington, Miss Mae.   Hickman Mills, Missouri: Rhoadschnell Presse Inc., 1965.

Silver, Diane. (ed.). *Kansas Storms* . Hillsboro, Kansas: Hearth Publishing, 1991.

Slaughter, Stephen. *History of a Missouri Farm Family: The O.V. Slaughters* . Harrison, New York: Harbor Hill Books, 1978.

Trimble, Vance H. *Sam Walton: Founder of Wal-Mart: The Inside Story of America's Richest Man*. New York: Penquin Company Dutton, 1990.

Turnbaugh, Jim and Aggie. *Twilight Twister*. Grandview, Missouri: Jackson County Advocate, 1957.

Weems, John Edward. *The Tornado* . New York: Doubleday and Company, Inc., 1977.

Kleinfelder, Rita Lang. *When We Were Young: A Babyboomer Yearbook*. New York: Prentice Hall, 1993.

ARTICLES

Bigler, Stuart G., Jackson, Robert. "Inside the Kansas City Tornado," *Weatherwise*, June 1958.

Lear, John. "How Stormy Weather Is Born," *Saturday Review*, July 4, 1959.

Lewis, Jack. "The Resurrection of Ruskin Heights," *American Mercury*, January 1959.

Taylor, Verta. "Good News About Disaster," *Psychology Today*, October 1977.

"New Terror In A Savage Spring," *Life*, June 3, 1957.

"Weather Notes," *Monthly Weather Report*, June 1957.

"Sometimes It Boils Over," *Saturday Review*, October 4, 1958.

"Tornadoes Break Record," *Science News Letter*, June 22, 1957.

"Predicting A Tornado," *Time*, June 27, 1955.

"Caught in the Suburbs," *Time*, June 3, 1957.

NEWSPAPERS

Kansas City Star, Sunday January 25, 1953.

Kansas City Star, Sunday May 19, 1957.

Kansas City Times, Monday May 20, 1957.

Kansas City Star, Monday May 20, !957.

Kansas City Times, Tuesday May 21, 1957.

Kansas City Star, Tuesday May 21, 1957.

Kansas City Times, Wednesday May 22, 1957.

Kansas City Star, Wednesday May 22, 1957.

Kansas City Times, Thursday May 23, 1957.

Kansas City Star, Thursday May 23, 1957.

Kansas City Times, Friday May 24, 1957.

Kansas City Star, Friday May 24, 1957.

Kansas City Times, Saturday May 25, 1957.

Kansas City Star, Saturday May 25, 1957.

Kansas City Star, Sunday May 26, 1957.

Kansas City Times, Monday May 27,1957.

Kansas City Star, Monday May 27, 1957.

Kansas City Star, Sunday June 16, 1957.

Kansas City Star, Wednesday June 19, 1957.

Kansas City Star, Thursday September 26, 1957.

Kansas City Star, Wednesday November 20, 1957.

Kansas City Star, Sunday May 18, 1958.

Kansas City Star, July 5, 1959.

Kansas City Star, Sunday May 20, 1962.

Kansas City Star, Sunday May 21, 1967.

Kansas City Star, Wednesday May 19, 1982.

Kansas City Southland Star, May 20, 1987.

Jackson County Advocate , Thursday May 23, 1957.

Jackson County Advocate , Thursday May 30, 1957.

Jackson County Advocate , Thrusday June 6, 1957.

Independence Examiner, Tuesday May 21, 1957.

Independence Examiner, Wednesday May 22, 1957.

Independence Examiner, Thursday May 23, 1957.

Independence Examiner, Monday May 27, 1957.

ADDITIONAL SOURCES

Aftermath of A Kansas City Tornado Dun and Bradstreet Newsletter, summer 1957.

Annual Report. Menorah Medical Center, Kansas City, Missouri, 1956-1957.

The Bendix News. Bendix Aviation Corporation, Kansas City, May 1957.

Buildings To Be Dedicated Consolidated School District #1,1957.

Collier, Rev. Harry Dale. *News For Church and Home.* The Ruskin Heights Presbyterian Church, May 20, 1957.

Confidence Justified: A Pictorial Report. The Salvation Army, Kansas City, June 1957.

Congressional Record. Federal-State-Local Cooperation on Tornado and Flood Disasters in Missouri. Speech of Hon. Stuart Symington in the Senate of the United States. Washington ,D.C., July 9, 1957.

Disaster Postscripts. American Red Cross, Kansas City and Jackson County Chapter, August 1957.

Glenn, William. Personal letter to relatives, May 27, 1957.

Hickman Mills History. Hickman Mills Chamber of Commerce, 1965.

Hourly Observations. National Severe Storm Forecast Center, Kansas City, Missouri, May 20, 1957.

Mass Meeting. Residents meeting for Ruskin Heights tornado victims, May 25, 1957.

Panoramic View of the Lost Township Hickman Mills, Missouri.

Radar Weather Observations U.S. Department of Commerce, Weather Bureau, May 1957.

Ruskin Heights Tornado Memorial. Ruskin Heights Homes Association, May 18, 1958.

Session Minutes. Ruskin Heights Presbyterian Church, May 21, 1957.

Tornado Dinner. Hickman Mills Chamber of Commerce Recognition Dinner program, September 19,1957.
Williams, Richard J. *Kansas City Tornadoes.* National Severe Storms Forecast Center Kansas City, Missouri, 1984.

Williams, Richard J. *Kansas City Tornadoes.* National Severe Storms Forecast Center Kansas City, Missouri, 1984.

Tornadoes!! The Entity. (Videocassette) Norman Beerger Productions, Inc., 1993.

Tornado Video Classics. (Videocassette) Environmental Films, 1994.

Tornado Video Classics: Volume Two (Videocassette) Environmental Films, 1994.

Bodine, Walt. *Diary Of A Disaster.* (radio broadcast) Marr Sound Archive, Kansas City, Missouri, May 24,1957.

NAME INDEX